Dedicated to the unseen hands that hide throughout this work...

HOME SCIENCE EXAM COMPANION - A COMPREHENSIVE GUIDE

FOR HIGHER SECONDARY XII HOME SCIENCE STUDENTS

TREESA SINDHU P. THOMAS

Made with ♥ on the Notion Press Platform
www.notionpress.com

Contents

Preface

Welcome to the fascinating world of Home Science! This guide is designed to be a comprehensive resource for understanding and mastering the diverse subjects within Home Science.

Home Science is an integrated field of Nutrition, Human development, Family resource management, Textiles, and Extension education. Its relevance goes beyond the curriculum of classroom study, as it touches every facet of our lives. It is through the in-depth study of Home Science that we learn to make our living much healthier, efficient, and more aesthetically living environments. Our goal is to make complex topics accessible and engaging, encouraging you to apply what you learn in meaningful ways.

As you embark on this journey through Home Science, we encourage you to approach each chapter with curiosity and an open mind. The skills and knowledge you acquire will not only benefit you personally but also contribute to the well-being of your family and community.

Thank you for choosing this guide.

Happy learning and living!

Treesa Sindhu P. Thomas

CHAPTER I

Basic Nutrition

1. Anti-aging vitamin is...........

a) **Vitamin E** b) Vitamin K c) Vitamin C d) Vitamin A

2. Pick the odd one out

a) Vitamin A b) Vitamin D c) Vitamin E d) **Vitamin C**

3. Identify water soluble vitamin from the following:

(a) Vitamin A (b) **Vitamin** C (c) Vitamin D (d) Vitamin E

4. Choose calcium deficiency disease:

(a) Scurvy (b) **Osteoporosis** (c) Anaemia (d) Goitre

5. Name the disease caused by the deficiency of Iron.

(a) Scurvy (b) Rickets (c) **Anaemia** (d) Marasmus

6. Fill in the blank:

Mono Saccharides, Disaccharides, ... **(Poly saccharides)**

7. Beri-Beri is a disease caused by a deficiency of _____.

a) **Thiamine** (B) Riboflavin (c) Niacin (d) Pyridoxin

8. One gram of protein provides ________ k cal of energy.

(a) 4.3 (b) **5.56** (c) 9.3 (d) 3.6

9. Find out the disease caused by the deficiency of Vitam in-D.

(a) **Rickets** (b) Night blindness (c) Scurvy (d) Anaemia

10. Match the following:

Carbohydrate - Anaemia (2)
Iron - Infantile scurvy (3)
Vitamin C - Oedema (4)
Water - Marasmus (1)

11. What are macronutrients?

(a) carbohydrates, protein, minerals (b) vitamins, fat, protein
(c) vitamins, minerals (d) **carbohydrates, protein, fat**

12. Which of the following food components give energy to our body?

(a) Proteins (b) Vitamins (c) Minerals **(d) Carbohydrates**

13. Which of the following food items provides dietary Fiber?

(a) Pulses (b) Wholegrain (c) Fruits and vegetables (d) **All of the above**

14. Which of the following food products are the best sources of animal proteins?

(a) Milk (b) Egg (c) Cheese (d) **All of the above.**

15. Which of the following mineral functions by building strong bones and teeth?

(a) Iodine (b) **Calcium** (c) Iron (d) Sodium

16. Egg is a rich source of __________.

(a) Proteins (b) Vitamins (c) Minerals (d) **All of the above**

17. Which of the following food items is the best source of plant proteins?

(a) Milk (b) Egg (c) **Legumes** (d) Cheese

18. Guava, Lemon, Orange and Tomato are rich in ___________.

(a) vitamin A (b) vitamin B **(c) vitamin C** (d) vitamin D

19. Potatoes, cereals, beans, pulses and oats are rich in ___________.

(a) Proteins (b) Vitamins (c) Minerals (d) **Carbohydrates**

20. Which of the following is the most essential nutrient for a woman during her initial stages of pregnancy to prevent birth defects?

(a) Thiamine (b) **Folic acid** (c) Vitamin C (d) Vitamin E

21. Which of the following vitamin helps in blood clotting?

(a) Vitamin A (b) Vitamin C (c) Vitamin D (d) **Vitamin K**

22. Which of the following vitamin deficiency causes Beriberi?

(a) **Vitamin B1** (b) Vitamin B2 (c) Vitamin B6 (d) Vitamin B12

23. Which of the following nutrient deficiency causes megaloblastic anaemia?

(a) **Folic acid** (b) Niacin c) Pyridoxine (d) Cobalamin

24. Which of the following is a fat-soluble vitamin?

(a) Vitamin B (b) Vitamin C (c) Vitamin B_{12} (d) **Vitamin K**

25. Which of the following diseases is caused by the deficiency of Niacin?

(a) Scurvy (b) Rickets (c) **Pellagra** (d) Pernicious anaemia

26. Which of the following vitamins is also known as cobalamin?

(a) Vitamin B11 (b) Vitamin B2 (c) Vitamin B6 (d) **Vitamin B12**

27. Which of the following minerals controls growth and body weight?

(a) **Iodine** (b) Calcium (c) Phosphorous (d) All of the above

28. Which of the following vitamins are called fat-soluble vitamins?

(a) vitamin B (b) **vitamin E** (c) vitamin C (d) vitamin B2

29. Which is the leading cause of blindness in children worldwide?

(a) Glaucoma (b) Cataracts (c) Colour blindness (d) **Vitamin A deficiency**

30. The natural source of vitamin D is:

(a) **Sunshine** (b) Spinach (c) Apples (d) Vitamin D supplements.

31. .... is ‘a state of complete physical, mental and social wellbeing. **(Health)**

32. Name the disease caused by the deficiency of Iron.

(a) Scurvy (b) Rickets (c) **Anaemia** (d) Marasmus

32. 1 gram of fat supplies ----------- K Cals of energy. **(9.3)**

33. Grey coloured spots in triangular shapes are located in the conjunctiva during vitamin A deficiency. This is called..................

(a) **Bitot’s spots** (b) Dementia (c) Cretinism (d) Phrynoderma

34. The normal iron requirement of an adult woman is

(a) 35 mg (b) 1200 mg (c) **21 mg** (d) 600 mg

35. A normal healthy person has .... mg of glucose in 100 ml of blood **(80-120)**

36. Which of the following is not a deficiency disease of calcium

(a) Osteoporosis (b) Tetany (c) **Kwashiorkar** (d) Osteomalacia

37. Identify anti haemorrhagic vitamin

(a) Vitamin A (b) Vitamin C (c) Vitamin B (d) **Vitamin K**

• • •

Short answer questions and answers

1. Define Nutrition

Nutrition may be defined as the combination of processes by which the living organism receives food, digests it, absorbs, and utilizes its contents for growth, maintenance, and repair of the body.

2. Define Optimum nutrition

Optimal nutrition occurs when all vital nutrients are available in the right amounts, necessary for the human body. Health, happiness, productivity and long life are achieved through optimum nutrition. The signs of optimum nutrition include: normal height for age, age weight, clear complexion, vibrant skin appearance, good hair color and texture, healthy pink nails and proper posture.

3.Write a short note on Malnutrition

Malnutrition refers to an undesirable intake of food and nutrients that leads to poor health. It may be due to deficiency, excess or imbalance of nutrients in the diet. malnourishment is of two types Under nutrition and over-nutrition. Malnourishment is when there are not enough essential nutrients in the body. Over-nutrition means eating too much of one or more nutrients creating a strain on body processes.

• • •

4. Define nutrients

They are defined as the constituents in food that enable us to carry out body functions. Nutrients are constituents of food, which the body must require for growth, reproduction and leading a healthy life.

5. Describe the deficiency disorders associated with calcium

- **Osteoporosis**: This is a sickness that occurs mostly in middle-aged and elderly women where there is decrease in the bone mass of skeleton.
- **Osteomalacia**: Osteomalacia is a condition in which the quality, but not the quantity, of bone is reduced.
- **Tetany**: This happens when calcium falls below critical level in blood.

6. List the functions of Iodine.

- Thyroxin is produced by thyroid gland. Thyroxin helps in carbohydrate metabolism.
- Thyroxin is necessary for normal skeletal and physical development.
- Iodine helps tissues to consume oxygen.

7. Differentiate between goitre and cretinism

Deficiency of Iodine in adults is called goitre. The thyroid gland enlarges to overcome the deficiency and this causes the swelling known as simple or colloid goitre. Deficiency of Iodine in children is called cretinism. In children, severe iodine deficiency may result in retardation of growth. This condition is known as cretinism

7. Enlist the functions of Vitamin A

- It is essential for building cells
- It enables growth of all cells especially of skeletal cells
- It helps normal tooth formation
- It is essential for the normal reproductive function in males
- It plays a major role in maintaining normal vision
- It plays an important role in maintaining the myelin sheath of nervous tissues
- It is also known as anti-infective vitamin, as it provides resistance to infection.

8. List the symptoms of Marasmus.

- Severe growth retardation
- Loss of subcutaneous fat and severe muscle wasting
- The child looks appallingly thin and limbs appear as skin and bones
- Shrivelled body, Bony prominence
- Wrinkled skin
- Failure to thrive, Irritability, fretfulness and apathy
- Frequent watery diarrhoea and acid stools and dehydration

9. Briefly explain the deficiency disorders associated with Vitamin A in the body

- **Night blindness:** lack of vitamin A can cause difficulties in adjusting from bright to dark environments. This happens because the production of a substance called rhodopsin is not as efficient. As a result, the ability to see in low light conditions is reduced, and if left untreated, it can lead to a condition called xerophthalmia. When this happens, the conjunctiva, the clear membrane covering the eye, becomes dry and loses its shine. The eye loses its transparent appearance and becomes grey and cloudy.
- **Bitots Spots:** Grey coloured spots in triangular shapes are located in the conjunctiva during vitamin A deficiency. This is called Bitot's spots.
- **Phrynoderma:** In vitamin A deficiency, the skin becomes rough due to the damage of epithelial cells. This condition is known as follicular keratosis or toad skin or phrynoderma.

10. Differentiate between Osteomalacia and rickets

Osteomalacia and rickets are both bone softening disorders caused by the deficiency of vitamin D. The main difference between the two is that rickets is more common in kids, while osteomalacia tends to affect adults. In osteomalacia, the person might experience bone pain, weakness in muscles, and trouble walking. Basically, osteomalacia is like rickets for grown-ups.

11. Explain the deficiency diseases of Thiamine.

Clinically, thiamine deficiency can be classified into three types:

- **Infantile Beriberi:** Due to maternal thiamine deficiency, infantile beriberi occurs during the first few months of life. The symptoms include vomiting, green-coloured diarrhea, oedema, loss of appetite, and restlessness.

- **Dry Beriberi**: This is characterized by the involvement of the peripheral nerves of the legs and arms. Numbness in the ankles and tenderness in the calf muscles are the symptoms.
- **Wet Beriberi**: One has dry beri beri with oedema.

12. Write a note on dehydration and oedema

- **Dehydration**: When the intake of water and other fluids is less than what the body needs. Dehydration is caused by excessive loss of water due to vomiting, diarrhoea, and perspiration. Any loss of fluid in excess of 10 percent can be dangerous.
- **Oedema**: Oedema refers to the accumulation of excessive fluid in tissues. It occurs due to an increase in the amount of sodium in the extra-cellular fluid. The kidneys are unable to excrete sodium, and thus water is retained along with excess sodium and consequently causes oedema.

13. Identify and explain the deficiency of Niacin.

- **Pellagra**: Nicotinic acid deficiency is the cause of a disease named pellagra. It is associated with three D's: Dermatitis, Diarrhea, and Dementia.
- **Dermatitis:** There are marked changes only in the skin, particularly in the area exposed to sunlight and friction areas like elbows, surfaces of arms, and knees. Lesions are symmetrically distributed in affected parts. At first, there is reddening, thickening, and pigmentation of the skin. Later on, there is exfoliation leading ultimately to the parchment of skin, giving it a butterfly-like appearance.
- **Diarrhoea**: Diarrhoea exaggerates the deficit state. Structural defects, as well as absorptive defects of the small intestine, are present.
- **Dementia**: Characterized by irritability, depression, decreased concentration, and loss of memory.

14. Describe Scurvy

- The prolonged deficiency of ascorbic acid produces a disease condition called ' **scurvy**' in infants as well as adults.

- **Infantile scurvy** - Anorexia, failure to thrive, irritable. There is defective growth of bones. Haemorrhage occurs under the skin. Defective formation of teeth and gums become swollen.
- **Adult Scurvy**-General symptom is fever, susceptibility to infection, and delayed wound healing. Gums becomes spongy and bleeds easily- Gums becomes swollen and ulcerated. Blood vessels become fragile and porous due to defective formation of collagen. Joints becomes swollen and tender-Clinical symptoms appears when total body pool of ascorbic acid decreases. Skin becomes rough and dry.

15. Enumerate the functions of water.

- It serves as a building material to each cell of the body
- It is a universal solvent, capable of dissolving all the products of digestion
- It helps in the transportation of the products of digestion in the appropriate organs.
- It is required for many chemical reactions taking place in our body.
- It acts as a lubricant and prevents friction between the moving parts of the body.
- The body temperature is regulated through the evaporation of water from the skin and lungs.

16. Write a short note on PEM.

Protein-energy malnutrition, or PEM, is the condition of lack of energy due to a deficiency in all macronutrients and many micronutrients. It may develop suddenly or gradually. And can be described as mild, moderate, or severe. The symptoms of protein energy malnutrition or PEM are as follows: Apathy and irritability, the patient becomes weak and inefficient, impaired cognition and consciousness, temporary lactose deficiency, diarrhoea, causes amenorrhea in women, weight loss, shrinking of muscles, the skin gets thin, pale, dry, inelastic and cold, hair fall, impaired wound healing etc.

6 Marks questions and Answers

17. List the symptoms of Kwashiorkor

Kwashiorkor is one of the serious forms of PEM. It is seen most frequently in children of one to three years, but it may occur at any age. It is found in children who have a diet that is usually insufficient in energy and protein and often in other nutrients.

- Body weight is low despite oedema indicative of growth failure and some amount of muscle wasting which is masked by oedema
- Oedema first appears on the feet and legs and then spreads to the entire body. Face is puffy with sagging cheeks and swollen eyelids. Puffiness of oedema resembles moon face
- Mental development affected. Mental changes like apathy and irritability are common.
- The skin is scaly pigmented and the hair becomes thin, dry and brownish or reddish
- Anorexia is common in making it difficult to feed the child
- Diarrhoea may occur due to defective digestion and absorption. Deficiencies of vitamin A and B complex are observed.

18. Enumerate the functions of Dietary Fibre in our body

- Prevention of constipation: Fibre gives bulk and softness to the stool, which enables it to much more easily pass out of the body.
- Prevents and helps to cure different diseases of the digestive system.
- Fibres have therapeutic benefits in irritable bowel syndrome.
- Dietary Fibre helps maintain natural friendly bacteria in the large intestine.
- High Fibre food indirectly influences in weight control. They promote the feeling of fullness and satisfaction.

1.Explain the different dimensions of health

1. **Physical dimension**: A state in which every cell and every organ in body works at optimum capacity and in perfect harmony with rest of the body.
2. **Mental dimension**: State of balance between the individual and surrounding world and a harmony between oneself and others.
3. **Social dimension**: Harmony and integration between an individual and other members of society and with the world he inhabits.
4. **Spiritual dimension**: Spiritual health refers to that feature of a person searching for meaning and purpose in life.
5. **Emotional dimension**: Emotional health refers to feelings. This dimension reflects emotional aspects of humanness.

• • •

2. Draw the classification of proteins and explain each.

Based on the proportion of amino acids, proteins are classified into complete proteins, partially complete proteins and incomplete proteins. (illustration)

i. **Complete protein** (first class protein/ high biological value) contains a good proportion of all essential amino acids to promote the normal growth rate and to maintain the body. example. proteins in milk, fish, egg etc.
ii. **Partially complete protein** (proteins of lower biological value) – these proteins lack sufficient amount of some essential amino acids. These proteins can maintain life. example. plant proteins like dhal and cereals.
iii. **Incomplete proteins-** These are proteins completely lack one or more essential amino acids, example. gelatin and zein of corn.

3. Illustrate the classification of carbohydrates and explain each. Explain the functions of carbohydrates.

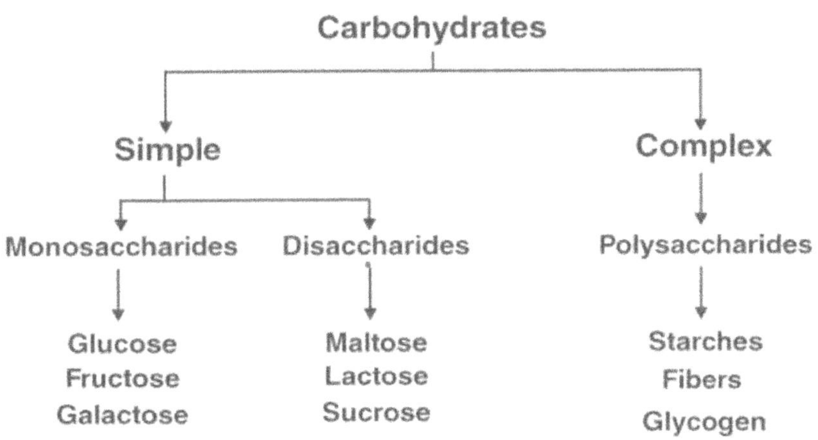

Classification of Carbohydrates

Carbohydrates are classified into three major groups:

- **Monosaccharides**: These are simple sugars. Only in this form our body absorbs CHO. Common examples include glucose, fructose, and galactose.

- **Disaccharides:** These consist of two monosaccharide units. It has to be converted to monosaccharide form for the body to absorb. Sucrose (table sugar) is a well-known disaccharide. Example: Sucrose (glucose + fructose), lactose (glucose + galactose), and maltose (glucose + glucose).
- **Polysaccharides:** These are long chains of monosaccharide units. These consist of more than three monosaccharide units.Our body cannot digest them. Examples include starch, cellulose, and glycogen.

Functions of Carbohydrates

1. **Energy Production** - The most important function of carbohydrate is to supply energy for the body. 1 gm of carbohydrate provides 4.3 K Cals of energy.
2. **Energy Storage** - If the body already has enough energy to support its functions, the excess glucose is stored as glycogen (the majority of which is stored in the muscles and liver).
3. **Protective function** - Carbohydrates have a protective and detoxifying action on the liver. Toxic substances produced by bacterial action are removed from the liver by glycogen.
4. **Heart health and diabetes** - Carbohydrate is used by the heart for muscular activities. Glycogen stored in the heart muscle is used for this purpose especially in an emergency. Dietary fibre helps in reducing blood sugar levels.
5. A continuous supply of glucose is essential for nervous tissues to function normally.
6. **Protein Sparing** - Protein is another important nutrient in our body with special functions. If enough carbohydrate is not present in the diet, then protein is used for energy purposes. This function of carbohydrate to spare protein for energy purposes, is known as protein sparing action.
7. **Synthesis of amino acids** - Carbohydrate is used by the body in the synthesis of non-essential amino acids.
8. **Lipid metabolism** - glucose additionally has a “fat-sparing” effect. This is because an increase in blood glucose stimulates release of the hormone insulin, which tells cells to use glucose (instead of lipids) to make energy. Carbohydrate is essential for the oxidation of fat. Excess carbohydrate is converted to fat.
9. Carbohydrate provides flavour and variety to the diet. It also retains water content in the colon. Cellulose adds bulk to the diet.

4. Analyse the functions of lipids.

- **Storing energy**: Fat is high in calorie (energy). One gram of fat supplies 9.3 K cals
- Fats carries fat-soluble vitamins like vitamin A, D, E and K.
- Fats have a protein sparing action
- Fats contain essential fatty acids
- **Insulating and Protecting** - Adipose tissue where fat is stored serves as an insulation material. Adipose tissue protects the vital organs too
- **Fat promotes growth**. It also enables proper sexual maturity
- **Provides Smell and taste to food** - Fats provide flavour and palatability to food. Food prepared in fat enhances satiety.

5. Describe the functions of proteins.

- **Growth and Maintenance**: Proteins are the building blocks of our body. The most important function of protein is to supply amino acids to the cells for the continuous replacement throughout life.
- **Provides Energy:** When the diet is insufficient in carbohydrates and fats for fuel, proteins are used to give energy for the body. Proteins provide 5.56 KCal of energy.
- **Provides Structure** - Some proteins are fibrous and provide cells and tissues with stiffness and rigidity. These proteins include keratin, collagen and elastin, which help form the connective framework of certain structures in your body
- Protein with iron forms haemoglobin in the blood. Haemoglobin carries oxygen to the tissues and eliminates carbon dioxide from tissues.
- **Maintenance of fluid balance in the body**: Plasma proteins like globulin and albumin regulates osmotic pressure and water balance in the body.
- **Synthesis of enzymes, hormones and digestive juices**: Proteins supply raw materials to the body for the synthesis of enzymes like pepsin and trypsin. Hormones like insulin and thyroxine are protein in nature. Digestive juices and antibodies are protein in nature.
- **Maintains Proper pH** - Protein plays a vital role in regulating the concentrations of acids and bases in your blood and other bodily fluids
- **Bolsters Immune Health** - Proteins help form immunoglobulins, or antibodies, to fight infection

Things to remember

- 1 gram Carbohydrate provides – **4.3** K Cals of energy
- 1 gram Protein provides – **5.56** K Cals of energy
- 1 gram Lipid provides – **9.3** K Cals of energy

Abbreviations

- **WHO** - World Health Organization
- **PEM** - Protein Energy Malnutrition

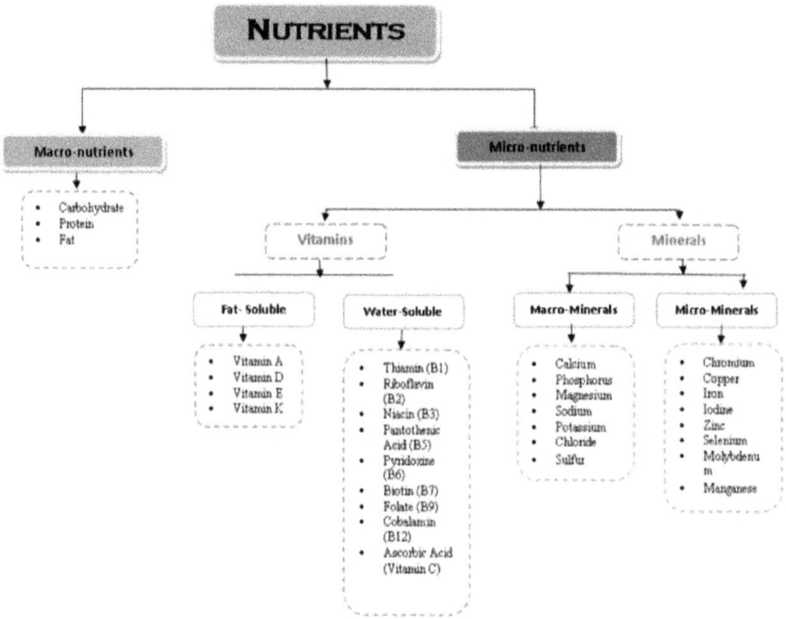

Classification of nutrients

Vitamins	**Other Name**	**Deficiency Diseases**
Fat Soluble vitamins (ADEK)		
Vitamin A	Retinol	Night blindness
Vitamin D	Calciferol Sunshine Vitamin	Rickets
Vitamin E	Anti- aging Anti sterility	Affects reproduction
Vitamin K	Phylloquinone Blood Clotting	Excessive bleeding due to injury
Water Soluble vitamins (BC)		
Vitamin B1	Thiamine	Beri-Beri
Vitamin B2	Riboflavin	Retarded growth, bad skin
Vitamin B3	Niacin	Pellagra
Vitamin B6	Pyridoxine	Anaemia
Vitamin B9	Folate or Folic Acid	Megaloblastic anaemia Neural tube defects
Vitamin B12	Cyanocobalamin	Anaemia
Vitamin C	Ascorbic acid	Scurvy
Minerals		
Iodine		Goitre, Cretinism
Calcium		Osteoporosis, osteo Malacia, tetani
Iron		Anaemia

Vitamins and Minerals chart

CHAPTER II

A Guide to Healthy Living

1 Mark Questions and Answers

1. ICMR- **Indian Council of Medical Research**

2. A gentle cooking method in which large pieces of food are cooking in a small amount of liquid just below simmering.

(a)Boiling (b) simmering (c) **poaching** (d) steaming

3. To cover small pieces of food completely with a liquid and simmer slowly in a covered pan.

(a) Simmering (b) **Stewing** (c) **poaching** (d) steaming

4. A cooking method that uses a small amount of fat in a skillet and used for larger pieces of food.

(a) **Frying** (b) sauteing (c) deep-fat frying (d) pan-broiling

5. A process in which foods are immersed in hot fat, without making contact with the cooking vessel.

(a) Boiling (b) steaming (c) frying (d) **deep-fat frying**

6. Small pieces of food are stirred constantly and cooked quickly over high heat in a small amount of oil until just tender.

(a) Sauteing (b) pan-broiling (c) **stir-frying** (d)braising

7. What is the main purpose of cooking food?

(a) To improve its taste (b) To make it safe to eat (c) To preserve it for longer periods (d) **Allof the above**

8. Which vitamin is most susceptible to destruction during cooking?

(a) Vitamin A (b) Vitamin C (c) Vitamin D (d) Vitamin E

9. The process of cooking food by dry heat in an oven is called:

(a) Boiling (b) **Baking** (c) Frying (d) Steaming

10. Which cooking method involves submerging food in a liquid at a relatively low temperature?

(a) Frying (b) Boiling (c) **Poaching** (d) Roasting

11. If sprouted green gram: Germination

Iodised salt: ....**(Fortification)**

12. Identify the cooking method, water is used as the cooking medium

(a) **Stewing** (b) baking (c) Deep fat frying (d) Pressure cooking

13. If boiling: water, Roasting: .... **(Air)**

14. Identify the process in which the sugars present in the food are broken into alcohol and carbon dioxide. **(fermentation)**

15. The Recommended Dietary Intake for Indians is suggested by the .... **(ICMR)**

16. Find the nutrient which is not enhanced by germination process

17. Iron (b) Folic acid (c) **Fat** (d) Vitamin C

• • •

Short answer questions and answers

1. Define Food pyramids

A food pyramid refers to a diagram of the number of servings of the basic food groups that should be taken daily. The major specific portions that are recommended for every food group are outlined in the pyramid as guidance towards having a balanced diet. The shape infers that more foods from the wider base of the pyramid—including bread, legumes, and vegetables—should be eaten than from the narrower top—which includes eggs, meat, and fish.

2. Write the general recommendations of food pyramid

- Eat a variety of foods to provide energy, proteins, vitamins, minerals, and Fibre for good health. Balance the food we eat with physical activity.
- Take a diet with plenty of grain products, a variety of vegetables, and fruits. These provide the necessary vitamins, minerals, Fibre and complex carbohydrates.

3. Enlist the objectives of cooking food

- **Improves the taste and quality**: It improves the natural flavor and texture of food. Eg. Roasting coffee seeds.
- **Destruction of microorganisms**: Cooking food to the required temperature for a required length of time can destroy all harmful microorganisms in food.
- **Improves digestibility**: Cooked food is easily chewed and swallowed. It is easily acted on by digestive juices.
- **Increases variety**: Through cooking, the same food items are made into different dishes.
- **Increases availability of nutrients:** Cooking increases the quality of protein by making some amino acids available to the body.

4. What are the principles of cooking

1. **To keep flavour in**- When actually food is cooked, aroma can be captured. Aroma makes the food taste better and it also encourages the flow of the digestive secretions for enhanced utilization of nutrients.
2. **To keep flavour out**- Sometimes food is cooked to remove its flavour into the gravy eg. mixed vegetable stew
3. **To gain the most nutritive value** through cooking we must employ the right procedures vitamins are particularly known to be destroyed by heat and much of those in C and B groups go together with minerals, minerals are also lost when cooking large quantities of water.

5. Write a short note on poaching. Enlist the advantages and disadvantages.

- Poaching, a culinary technique, involves cooking food in water just enough to submerge it at a temperature of 80-850C, which is less than the boiling point. The food usually made by this method is poached eggs, fish and fruits.
- Advantages - of poaching Very quick method of cooking Easily digestible since no fat is used. Disadvantages - of poaching Water soluble vitamins may be leached into the water

5. **Enlist the classification of food based on various food groups**

- Group I- cereal and grains
- Group II - Pulses and Legumes
- Group III - Milk & Meat Products
- Group IV - Fruits and Vegetables, Green Leafy Vegetables, Other Vegetables
- Group V - Fats and Sugars

6. **Nutrient loss is a consequence of all cooking processes. Explain any two**

- Boiling- During boiling, water soluble nutrients lost due to leaching.
- Poaching: During Poaching, water soluble nutrients are lost

- Simmering- in simmering, due to long time of cooking, heat sensitive nutrients missing

7. **Teenagers have worst food habits. explain**

- They sometimes skip meal
- Not proper timing in eating food Trying to reduce weight,
- teenagers sometimes dont eat food
- Less time
- Eating junk food and snacks instead of whole meal

8. **Briefly explain the method of Pressure cooking**

pressure cooking is the method of cooking food using steam under pressure and the equipment used is known as pressure cooker.

Advantages

- It takes less time to cook.
- Different items can be cooked at the same time.
- Fuel is saved.
- Requires less attention.
- Nutrient loss is less.

Disadvantages

- Need knowledge of using the equipment (pressure cooker) is required, otherwise accidents may occur.
- There may be mixing of flavours
- Food may get more soft than required.

9. **Differentiate Stewing and simmering**

- In stewing, food is cooked in a pan with a tight-fitting lid. Water will cover only half of the food. The food above the water is cooked by the steam generated within the pan. It is a slow method. Most vegetables and meat are prepared by this method.
- In simmering, food is cooked in a pan with well fit lid at temperature below boiling point of water (around 82 to 99 ^{0}C). This is a useful

method when food has to be cooked for long time to make it tender.

10. **Explain any two methods of cooking using water as the medium.**

- **Steaming**: Steaming is done by using boiling water and then using steam generated to cook food without water contact. Food is cooked at 100°C
- **Boiling**: Boiling is cooking food in water at 100°C and maintaining the water at that temperature till the food is made tender. When food items are cooked by boiling, food is first cooked at high temperature to break food and then brought down. boiling is the traditional method of cooking rice.

11. **Differentiate roasting and grilling**

- Roasting is traditionally cooking of meat in open fire. Nowadays, roasting is generally described as the cooking of meat or vegetables in the oven, added with hot fat to prevent drying and to enhance colour and flavour.
- In Grilling, the food is placed below or above or in between a red hot surface. Food is cooked by directly putting it to heat.

12. **Write notes on baking**

Baking is a method of cooking in which food gets cooked by hot air. Baked foods items are generally brown and crisp on the top, soft and porous at the centre. The temperatures that are normally used for baking are 120-2600C.

Advantages are: flavour and texture are improved. Variety of dishes can be made Uniform and bulk cooking can be achieved.

13. **Write the merits and demerits of microwave cooking**

In microwave cooking the food is heated using electromagnetic waves using the Microwave oven. The microwaves Emitted inside the oven are reflected by metal surface into food creating uniform heating of the food.

Advantages:

- Food is cooked very quickly.

- As the cooking time is less loss of nutrients will be less.
- Food gets cooked evenly.

Disadvantages:

- Specialized utensils are needed for cooking
- If the wrong time set, the food may get overcooked.
- Deep frying cannot be done.
- flavours may not blend well.

14. **What are the different methods of conservation of nutrients**

- Do not over soak pulses.
- Cook in minimum water.
- Wash vegetables before cutting
- Use minimum water to cook the vegetables
- Cover food while Cooking
- Avoid overcooking or reheating repeatedly.
- Serve cooked food immediately

15. Discuss the advantages of boiling.

- The simplest method of cooking.
- It does not require special skill and equipment
- Soluble starches can be removed, starch gets gelatinized and collagen gets hydrolysed
- Protein gets denatured
- Uniform cooking can be done.

16. Explain the advantages of pressure cooking.

- Food gets cooked easily with high temperature and pressure and thus saves fuel and time.
- Different items can be cooked at the same time.
- Requires less attention so less labour is required
- Nutrient or flavour loss is minimum due to less cooking time
- Hard foods are easily cooked
- Since steam loss is less, chances of burning or scorching are minimized

6 Marks Questions and Answers

17. Enlist the general guidelines for healthy living

- **Maintain regularity in routine**- Body can adapt to changes. But body is set to routine it is important to maintain it. Maintaining routine helps in sleeping well, eliminating bad habits and proper digestion.
- **Eat as much natural foods as possible**- Most natural foods are more nutritious than preserved foods. For example, a glass of fresh lime juice contains more vitamin C than lemon squash.
- **Adapt to seasonal variations**: Changes in seasons can affects our health. Diet should be modified so that body is not too much affected. For example during summer we should drink more water due to sweating.
- **Eat well**: Eat three to four meals a day but do not overeat. A meal should be eaten at the right time.

18. How is food classified According to the function?

Based on function food is classified in to: Energy yielding food, Body building food, Protective and Regulatory food.

- **Energy yielding Food**: Foods which provides energy to our body are called energy yielding foods. Our body needs energy to carry out life processes like respiration, circulation, digestion and absorption of nutrients. They are carbohydrates and fats. carbohydrates include cereals like rice, wheat, ragi. Fat sources are butter, ghee, vegetable oils like coconut oil, groundnut oil.
- **Body building food**: Protein is the important nutrient responsible for the repair and maintenance of tissues in the body. Foods rich in protein are called body building foods. Milk, meat, egg and fish are rich in proteins of high biological value.
- **Protective and regulatory food**: Foods rich in minerals and vitamins are known as protective and regulatory foods. They are essential for health and for the normal functioning of the human body and also protect from ill health and disease. Water is a regulatory food. Milk, egg, liver, fruits and green leafy vegetables are protective foods.

• • •

19. Explain the classification of food based on its keeping quality

20. Differentiate between Perishable and non – Perishable food with examples

- **Perishable food**- Perishable food have shorter life span. Perishable food items are easily damaged due to their high water content, bacterial action and enzymatic reaction. Vegetables and fruits, milk and milk products, eggs, fish are easily damaged unless properly preserved
- **Non perishable food**: Non perishable food items lack water content and hence microbial action is not possible in them. The shelf life of food products can be increased by using proper sanitation procedures during storage. Cereal grains, flours, legumes and pulses, spices, sugar and jaggery etc. if stored properly last for several months.

18. What are the different ways of nutrient loss during cooking ?

- **Over washing**: water soluble vitamins may lost when over washed.
- **Over peeling**: vitamins and minerals lost due to over peeling.
- **Washing after cutting**: Water soluble vitamins and minerals of vegetables and fruits may lost when washed after cutting
- **Over soaking**: If pulses are soaked in water for too long i.e., more than 2-3 days, it can lead to severe food poisoning
- **During preparation**: Using excessive water for cooking and removing the excess water leads to the loss of water soluble vitamins and minerals.
- **Cooking uncovered**: water soluble nutrients may evaporate, if the container is not covered
- **Over frying**: All fat soluble vitamins A, D, E, and K are lost when fried for long time.
- **Reheating**: Reheating food after cooking also destroys nutrients.

18. **Pizzas, burgers and soft drinks are known as junk food. Explain the impacts of junk food on children. Or evaluate the disadvantages of consuming junk foods.**

- Junk foods are easily accessible in our daily life.
- Nowadays we replace our meal with junk foods.
- Junk foods cannot provide the nutrients that are required by the body. A whole meal with vegetables, fruits and cereals is a must for the body.

- Junk food contains artificial colours, sweeteners and many other harmful substances. Chemicals are added to make them more attractive and tastier.

Side effects of junk foods

- Obesity in children Junk food often creates damage to nerves, digestive organs, brain, liver, heart and kidneys.
- Sodium carbonate, tartaric acid used in fizzy drinks can damage mucous parts of intestines and lives.
- Soft drinks cause calcium depletion and cause bone damage.
- Use of trans-fats may result in heart diseases.
- More sugar consumption damages brain and results in emotional disturbance

19. Explain the different Methods of Enhancing Nutrient Availability in food

Germination- Pulses and grains are soaked overnight, usually for 8-16 hours in minimum water. Seeds become maximum size by absorbing water, they are tied to a moist muslin cloth, for another 12-24 hours in a warm well-lit place. This results in the sprouting of white shoots. Soya bean, green gram, black gram etc can be easily germinated.

Advantages:

- Vitamin C level increases.
- Proteins and carbohydrates become easily digestible.
- The food becomes softer, chewable and more digestible
- Niacin, riboflavin and folic acid content increases by 60-100%
- Fenugreek seeds lose bitterness.
- It also reduces cooking time.

Fermentation- The sugars present in the food are broken into alcohol and carbon dioxide. This process is called food fermentation. Making the mixture rise 2-3 cm and making it porous, spongy and sour. Curd and yeast are mostly used to ferment foods. Example : Idli, Dosa, Appametc.

Advantages

- The food becomes porous, light and digestible Vitamin C content increases.
- Thiamine, riboflavin and niacin content also doubles.
- Texture and flavour of foods are enhanced.

Combination: It is a process in which food from different food groups are mixed in one dish to enhance nutrients and get a better taste. This helps to increase nutrient content in food. The most common examples are combining pulses and cereals, rice and green gram, wheat and dal etc. eg. Idli, dosa mix.

Advantages

- It helps to provide a balanced diet to all family members.
- More variety can be brought to meals.
- Cereals, pulses and vegetables combined in a diet supply a very good quantity of proteins, minerals and carbohydrates
- Combination of cereal and milk improves the protein and calcium content of food.

Fortification: It is the addition of one or more essential nutrients to food, even when it is normally or not normally contained in the food. This is done for the purpose of preventing or correcting a nutrient deficiency. eg. Fortified atta, Iodised salt.

Advantages

- Fortified food items contain more micronutrients It helps to maintain nutrient availability in body.
- It improves the nutritional status of a large proportion of the general population.
- Food fortification is more cost effective than any other methods.

CHAPTER III

Nutrition for Self and Family

1 Mark Questions and Answers

1. Which of the following is NOT a factor affecting meal planning ?

(a) Food availability (b) Life-style (c) Season (d) **Referenceman**

2. Daily calcium requirement of a pregnant woman is ______.

(a) 800 mg (b) 1000 mg (c) **1200 mg** (d) 600 mg

3. Adolescent girl requires _______ of calcium per day.

(a) 600 mg (b) 500 mg (c) 1200 mg (d) **800mg**

4. The protein allowance recommended for an adult is ________ per kilogram body weight.

(a) **1 gm** (b) 60 gm (c) 100 gm (d) None of these

5. Expand the term RDA (**Recommended Dietary Allowances**)

6. What is the recommended dietary allowance of protein per day for an average adult Indian man?

(a) 40 grams (b) **60 grams** (c) 55 grams (d) 45 grams

7. How much calcium is recommended daily for an adult Indian woman?

(a) **600 mg** (b) 1000 mg (c) 400 mg (d) 800 mg

8. What is the recommended daily intake of Vitamin C for Indian adults?

(a) **40 mg** (b) 60 mg (c) 80 mg (d) 100 mg

9. For Indian children aged 1-3 years, what is the RDA of iron?

(a) **9 mg** (b) 7 mg (c) 5 mg (d) 11 mg

10. What is the additional protein requirement per day for an Indian pregnant woman?

(a) 10 grams (b) **23 grams** (c) 15 grams (d) 30 grams

11. How much extra iron is recommended daily for a lactating Indian woman?

(a) 10 mg (b) 35 mg (c) 25 mg (d) **15 mg**

12. The RDA for calcium during pregnancy for Indian woman is:

(a) **1200 mg** (b) 1000 mg (c) 800 mg (d) 600 mg

13. What is the increased calorie requirement per day for an Indian woman during the second trimester of pregnancy?

(a) **350 kcal** (b) 450 kcal (c) 300 kcal (d) 500 kcal

14. For lactating Indian women, the RDA of Vitamin C is:

(a) **80 mg** (b) 60 mg (c) 100 mg (d) 120 mg

15. What is the recommended daily intake of iron for Indian adolescent girls?

(a) **28 mg** (b) 21 mg (c) 17 mg (d) 14 mg

16. How much calcium is recommended daily for Indian adolescent girls?

(a) **800 mg** (b) 1000 mg (c) 1200 mg (d) 1300 mg

17. The RDA for protein for Indian adolescent girls is:

(a) 45 grams (b) 55 grams (c) 60 grams (d) **50 grams**

18. What is the recommended daily intake of Vitamin A for Indian adolescent girls?

(a) 600 mcg (b) **700 mcg** (c) 800 mcg (d) 900 mcg

19. For Indian adolescent girls, the RDA of Vitamin C is:

(a) 40 mg (b) 65 mg (c) **75 mg** (d) 85 mg

• • •

Short answer Questions and Answers

1. Define meal planning

Meal Planning is the technique of providing the family with meals that will meet the nutritional requirements. It can be defined as the implementation of the principles of nutrition in one's daily diet in an appetizing way.

2. Nutritional requirements of pregnant woman and lactating woman

- **Pregnant**
- Protein- 82.2 g/day
- Iron- 35 mg/ day
- Calcium- 1200 mg/day
- **Lactating woman**
- Protein- 77.9 g/day
- Iron- 25 mg/day
- Calcium- 1200 mg/day

3. List the importance of meal planning.

- Fulfil the nutritional needs of all members of the family
- Serve well planned and attractive meals
- Make the food economical
- Cater to the food preferences of individual members of the family

- Save energy, time and money
- Use left over food
- Combine different food to increase the nutrient content.

4. How will you bring variety in meals?

- **Selection of food from different food groups**: to make them balanced and acceptable to the family members.
- **Variety in colour combinations**: Blending of different colours make food attractive and appetizing. Food appears dull if it is of the same colour.
- **Variety in texture**: Texture of food refers to the state of being soft, solid, crisp or liquid. Example: Contrasting textures with vegetables, juicy fruits and crispy bites. crispy food like pappads, chips etc., soft food like pudding, dal etc. and liquid food like rasam, buttermilk etc.
- **Variety in taste and flavour**: Meal should contain different tastes like salty, sour, sweet and pungent. Taste differences occur when sour foods like lemon, oranges and tomatoes are used. Bitter food like bitter gourd may be prepared into crispy bites.

5. Differentiate between reference man and reference woman

- A **reference man** is between 20-39 years of age and weighs 60 kg. He is free from disease and physically fit for active work. On each working day he is employed for eight hours in occupation that involves moderate activity. While not at work he spends eight hours in bed, 4-6 hours sitting and moving around, and two hours in walking and in active recreation or in household duties.
- A **reference woman**, is between 20-39 years of age, healthy and weighs 55 kg. She may be engaged for eight hours in general household work, in light industry or other moderately active work. Apart from eight hours in bed, she spends 4-6 hours sitting or moving around only through light activity, and two hours in walking or in active recreation or in household duties.

6. Explain any three factors affecting RDA.

1. **Age** (child/adolescent): A growing child requires more calories and protein per kilogram body weight than an adult. A growing adolescent boy may require more nutrients in terms of calories, proteins, minerals and vitamins compared to an adult officer or a retired teacher.
2. **Sex** (male/female): Girls require more iron than boys at the onset of menarche.
3. **Body size and frame**: A tall well-built man needs more calories than a small statured man because of his larger body surface area and the greater weight of his bones.

7. Describe the factors that affect meal planning. (any three)

- **Economic factor** - Foods such as milk, meat, fruits, nuts etc. are costly. However alternative sources like toned milk, seasonal and locally available fruits and vegetables, which are low cost and at the same time nutritious can be used.
- **Season** - Meals should be in accordance with the season. With the change in season, the availability of foodstuffs and our tastes also change. Seasonal food is more nutritious and preferable.
- **Food availability** - A maximum use of locally produced foodstuffs should be made because they are cheap, tasty and compatible with the climate.

6 Marks Questions and Answers

8. Explain any three principles of meal planning.

a. **To bring nutritional value**: A family consists of members of various age groups and physiological states. The nutritional requirement for each person varies. In order to get the required nutrients in the correct proportion, food from various food groups should be included in the diet.
b. **To consider personal preferences and food habits**: Families differ in their nutritional needs, number of family members, their likes and dislikes, number of meals taken etc. Food should be in accordance with the requirement of the different members of the family. It can be served to meet the requirements of each person by making few changes in the meal. **(Explain food habits of the family members affect meal planning)**

c. **To bring variety in meals:** Even if the food is tasty or nutritious, we do not like to eat the same food every day. Variety in food is a must so that all members of the family enjoy it. This can be ensured by selecting food from various food groups, by blending colours, flavours, textures and by using different cooking methods.

9. Explain the various factors influencing RDA

- *Sex* – In general requirement is more for men than women.
- ***Age***– Adult men and women require nutrients for maintenance whereas infants and children require it for growth and maintenance. Nutrient requirements during childhood are proportional to growth rate.
- ***Body weight:*** Among adults' requirements are related to body weight and size.
- ***Physiological states***- During menstruation, pregnancy and lactation women require some nutrients more than the normal times.
- ***Requirements of sports persons and athletes*** who perform high levels of extreme activity are high sometimes 2-3 times the normal times.
- ***Physical activity***- Sedentary person needs much less nutrients than a moderate to severely active person.
- ***Environment***- Extremes of climate or high altitude alters the need for certain nutrients.

10. Briefly Explain the nutritional requirements and plan a day's menu for an Indian pregnant woman

Nutritional Requirements for Indian Pregnant Women:

1. **Calories:** Increase daily calorie intake by approximately 350 calories (1900+350 = 2250 Kcals.)during pregnancy, especially in the second and third trimesters.
2. **Proteins:** The requirements of protein, in pregnancy increases by 27.2 g /day. Include lean meats, fish, poultry, eggs, beans, lentils, and cottage cheese (paneer).
3. **Carbohydrates:** Opt for whole grains like brown rice, whole wheat bread, and oats.
4. **Fats:** Consume healthy fats from nuts, seeds, and vegetable oils.
5. **Vitamins and Minerals:** Prioritize fruits, vegetables, and dairy products for essential nutrients. **Calcium:** Calcium requirement during pregnancy

is 1200 mg/ day. **Iron**: Iron requirement during pregnancy is 35 mg / day. Dates, lotus seeds, and green leafy vegetables are rich in iron. Zinc is required for DNA and RNA synthesis and cell development. All vitamins are required in additional quantities especially vitamin A, B complex, C, D and folic acid.

6. **DHA (Docosahexaenoic Acid)**: Found in walnuts and seafood, crucial for fetal brain development.

Sample Day's Menu:
Here's a balanced meal plan for an Indian pregnant woman:

- **Pre-Breakfast Snack (Around 7 AM)**:
  - A handful of soaked almonds or walnuts.
- **Breakfast (Around 9 AM)**:
  - Poha (flattened rice) or rava upma (semolina dish) with vegetables.
  - A glass of milk or a cup of herbal tea.
- **Mid-Morning Snack (11 AM to Noon)**:
  - A fruit (banana, apple, or orange).
- **Lunch (1.30 PM)**:
  - Roti (whole wheat flatbread) or brown rice.
  - Lentil curry (dal) with spinach (palak) or fenugreek (methi).
  - Vegetable curry (such as cauliflower, beans, or pumpkin).
  - A small portion of curd (yogurt).
- **Evening Snacks**:
  - A handful of roasted chana (chickpeas) or murmura (puffed rice).
- **Dinner (8 PM)**:
  - Vegetable pulao (rice cooked with mixed vegetables).

  - Grilled fish or paneer tikka (if vegetarian).
  - A side salad with cucumber, tomato, and carrot.

Remember to stay hydrated by drinking plenty of water throughout the day.

11. Nutritional requirement and plan a day's menu for an Indian lactating mother`

Nutritional Requirements for Indian Lactating Mothers:

1. **Calories:** the ICMR has recommended an additional 600 Kcal for 0-6 months and an additional 520 K cals from 7 to 12 months. For a sedentary worker would be 1900 + 600 = 2500 Kcal (0-6 months lactation) 1900 + 520 = 2420 Kcal (7-12 months lactation)
2. **Iron:** Essential for energy and blood production. Iron is not secreted much into the milk so the iron requirement during lactation is 25 mg/ day.
3. **Calcium:** Crucial for bone health and milk production. During lactation ICMR has prescribed 1200 mg of calcium for mother's milk production.
4. **Protein:** Supports tissue repair and milk synthesis. ICMR has recommended an additional daily intake of 22.9 gm for the first six months and 15.2 gm during 7-12 months of lactation.
5. **Vitamins and Minerals:** vitamins – especially vitamin B6 , B12, A and D. Vitamin C requirements are 80 mg per day considering the vitamin C secreted in human milk.
6. **Fat:** The level of fat in the diet would provide adequate energy to enable nursing women to meet their higher energy needs.
7. **Fluids:** A lactating mother must drink plenty of fluids (at least 2 litres a day) to protect herself from dehydration. A sensible rule of the thumb is to drink a beverage like soup, juice, milk or water at each meal and each time the baby nurses.

Sample Day's Menu:

Here's a balanced meal plan for an Indian lactating mother:

- **Pre-Breakfast Snack (Around 7 AM):**
- A handful of soaked almonds or walnuts.
- **Breakfast (Around 9 AM):**
- Ragi (finger millet) porridge or whole wheat upma with vegetables.

- A glass of milk or herbal tea.
- **Mid-Morning Snack (11 AM to Noon)**:
- A fruit (guava, orange, or apple).
- **Lunch (1.30 PM)**:
- Roti (whole wheat flatbread) or brown rice.
- Lentil curry (dal) with spinach (palak) or fenugreek (methi).
- Vegetable curry (such as cauliflower, beans, or pumpkin).
- A small portion of curd (yogurt).
- **Afternoon Snack (4 PM)**:
- A bowl of sprouts salad (moong or chana).
- **Dinner (8 PM)**:
- Vegetable pulao (rice cooked with mixed vegetables).
- Grilled fish or paneer tikka (if vegetarian).
- A side salad with cucumber, tomato, and carrot.

Remember to stay hydrated by drinking plenty of water throughout the day.

		Lactation	
Nutrients	**Pregnancy**	**0-6 months**	**6-12 months**
Energy	+350, +9.5 (2nd trimester +22.0(3rd Trimester)	+600	+520
Protein	82.2g	77.9g	70.2g
Calcium	1200 mg	1200 mg	1200 mg
Iron	35 mg	25 mg	25 mg
Vitamin C	60 mg	80 mg	80 mg
Vitamin A	800 ug	950 ug	950 ug

CHAPTER IV

Diet Therapy

1 Mark Questions and Answers

1. A moderately high fat diet is used in the treatment of............................(**Severe undernutrition**)

2. Write one disease condition in which high protein diet is prescribed (**fever**)

3. The four attributes of therapeutic diet are:

(a) Adequacy (b) .... (c) palatability (d).................... (**Accuracy, Economy**)

4. Analyse the following qualitative diet modification and name any one disease condition

High protein diet: .... (**Kwashiorkar, fever**)

Fat controlled diet: .... (**cardiovascular disease**)

5. Examine the disease conditions given below and suggest the qualitative modification of diet required:

(a) Gout:.........(**low calorie**) (b) Infective hepatitis:..........(**High protein**)

(c) Hypertension:.........(**low calorie**) (d) Gall bladder disease::.........(**low calorie**)

6. High protein diet is prescribed in ....

(a) After **surgery** (b) Atherosclerosis (c) Hepatic Encephalopathy

7. ORS is given to prevent..........

Dehydration (b) Fever (c) Constipation (d) Obesity

8. Select a condition in which a high fibre diet is prescribed from the following

a) Diarrhoea b) **Obesity** c) Hypertension d) Fever

9. High calorie diet is prescribed for ________.

(a) **Underweight** (b) Obesity (c) Diabetes (d) None of these

10. Complete it:

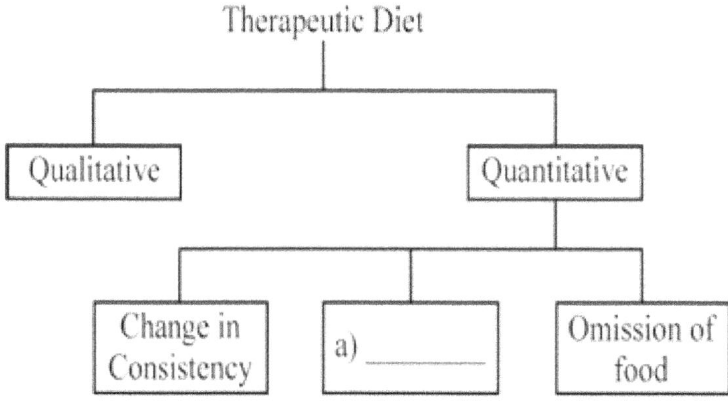

(Rearrangement of meals)

11. A person who is under-weight needs

(a) Low calorie diet (b) **High calorie diet** (c) Low protein diet (d) High fibre diet

12. **Diet required for following diseases**

- Gout- Low calorie diet
- Infective hepatitis- High protein diet
- Hypertension- Low calorie diet
- Gall bladder disease- Low calorie diet /fat controlled diet

Short Answer Questions and Answers

1. Define diet therapy

Diet therapy means implementing a specific diet (food and drink) not only for the care of the sick, but also for the prevention of diseases and maintenance of health.

2. List out the foods allowed during obesity

Vegetables like cucumber, tomato, green leafy vegetables Sprouted grams Wheat, barley Coffee or tea without sugar

3. List out the objectives of diet therapy

The general objectives of diet therapy are:

- To maintain a good nutritional status
- To correct nutrient deficiencies occurred due to the disease

- To afford rest to the whole body or to the specific organ affected by the disease
- To adjust food intake to suit the body's ability to metabolize the nutrients during disease
- To bring about changes in body weight whenever necessary

4. Enlist the attributes of therapeutic diet.
The four attributes of a therapeutic diet are:

- Adequacy
- Accuracy
- Economy
- Palatability.

5. Describe the Factors to be considered in planning therapeutic diets

1. The disease condition which requires a change in the diet
2. The possible duration of the disease
3. The factors in the diet which must be altered to overcome these conditions
4. The patients' tolerance for food

6. Explain any 3 qualitative modifications of diet

High calorie diet: This is a normal diet with an increase in the calorie level to 3000 calories or more. The diet may be modified in consistency and flavour, according to specific needs. These diets are prescribed for • underweight • fever • hyperthyroidism • burns.

- **Low calorie diet**: This is a normal diet with energy values reduced to 1500, 1200 or 1000 calories. Protein levels should be at 65 to 100 g. Supplements of vitamin A and thiamine should be provided. These diets are prescribed for weight reduction in • diabetes mellitus • cardiovascular diseases • hypertension • gout • gall bladder disease • preceding surgery.
- **Fat controlled diet**: The calories from fat should provide about 30% - 35% of the total calories with 10% from saturated fat and 12– 14% from poly-unsaturated fats. Usually fat controlled diets are prescribed for: • gall bladder diseases • atherosclerosis • myocardial infarction •

hyperlipidemia etc.

7. Differentiate between clear fluid diet and full fluid diet

- **Clear Fluid Diet**: A clear fluid diet is usually used for 1 or 2 days. The amount per feeding is 30 – 60 ml/hour. As the patient's tolerance improves, the amount can be increased. This diet is indicated in: • acute illness • surgery • gastrointestinal disturbances. Example: tea with lemon and sugar • coffee • fat free broths. • carbonated beverages • cereal waters.
- **Full fluid diet**: Full fluid diet includes food items which are liquid at room temperature. It is free from cellulose and irritating condiments. Six or more feedings can be given daily. The protein content of the diet can be increased by incorporating whole egg, egg white, non-fat dry milk in beverages and soups. The calorie value of the diet can be increased by adding butter to cereal gruels and soups, glucose in beverages and using creams in dessert. This diet is indicated when a patient is: • acutely ill • unable to chew or swallow solid food. Food allowed in a full fluid diet are: Beverages — Cocoa, coffee or tea.

8. Write a short note on high fibre diet

Dietary fibre plays a significant role in colonic function. High fibre diet is mainly used for constipation and diverticulosis. This is a normal diet with fibre increased to 15–20 mg. daily. Fluid intake is also increased. Concentrated food should be replaced by those of greater bulk. Food items which can be included in the diet are plenty of long fibred vegetables, salads, fruits and whole cereal grains.

9. Explain low residue diet

Low residue diet is made up of food which can be completely absorbed, thereby leaving a little or no residue for the formation of faeces. This diet provides insufficient minerals and vitamins and therefore it must be supplemented. Food high in fibre should be omitted. Food which contains residue but not fibre such as milk are also omitted or restricted. Strained fruits and vegetables without skins are usually permitted. Meat should be tender or ground to reduce connective tissue. The diet is usually used in • severe diarrhoea to afford rest to the gastrointestinal tract • ulcerative colitis in initial stages • surgeries • partial intestinal obstruction • Reducing the bulk in the gastrointestinal tract whenever necessary.

10. Explain the morphological classification of anaemia

1. **Normocytic anaemia**: In normocytic anaemia the size of the red blood cells and the haemoglobin content is normal. It occurs as a result of haemorrhage or when erythropoiesis is suppressed by ionizing rays or toxins.
2. **Macrocytic anaemia**: In macrocytic anaemia, the erythrocytes are abnormally large because they are saturated with haemoglobin. It is caused by the deficiency of vitamin B12 and folic acid deficiency.
3. **Microcytic anaemia**: This type of anaemia is characterised by the presence of erythrocytes which are smaller or normal and sometimes contain little haemoglobin. An example is anaemia due to the deficiency of iron.

11. What are the different types of fever

- **Short duration fever**: Such fever is acute but short in duration eg., common cold, cough, throat infection, influenza, measles, pneumonia etc.
- **Long duration fever**: Such fever lasts for longer duration with low temperature, eg. tuberculosis.
- **Intermittent fever**: Such fever occurs in intervals, eg. malaria, typhoid etc.

12. Define anaemia

Anaemia is a condition that develops when blood lacks enough healthy red blood cells or haemoglobin. Haemoglobin is the main part of red blood cells that binds oxygen.

6 Marks Questions and Answers

13. Explain the causes of diarrhoea

1. **Malnourishment**: diarrhoea is common in Protein-Energy malnutrition, vitamin deficiencies etc. the body is more susceptible to infections because of lower immunity and weak digestive system.
2. **Unhealthy environment**: Contaminated food and water are the main causes of diarrhoea. Flies are the carriers of this disease.
3. **Food allergy**: Sensitivity to a particular food is known as food allergy, eg., if a person is allergic to egg, spinach, brinjal; their intake may lead to

acute diarrhoea.

4. **Drugs**: Sensitive to certain drugs and the use of such drugs leads to diarrhoea, eg., sensitivity to antibiotics, drugs etc.
5. **Psychological factors**: The emotional sensitivity of a person in a particular situation can also be the cause of diarrhoea, eg., tension during an examination, immense happiness or sorrow etc.

14. Types of diarrhoea

1. **Acute diarrhoea**: It is caused by eating unhygienic, infected, and stale food. Its duration lasts for 1-3 days. It is characterized by loose, watery stools, abdominal pain, fever, vomiting and weakness in the body. Excessive loss of water from the body and may lead to dehydration.
2. **Chronic diarrhoea**: It lasts for a much longer period. It is caused by the intake of some irritant or stale food. Nutritional deficiencies may develop in chronic diarrhoea. Water electrolyte balance is also disturbed. There is the loss of water-soluble vitamins due to excessive loss of water from the body which may lead to vitamin deficiencies.

15. Briefly explain the nutritional requirements of a diarrhoea patient and plan a day's menu for diarrhoea patient

i. Energy: Considerable loss of energy demands sufficient intake of calories. To meet the calorie requirements, easily digestible carbohydrate rich food like fruit juices, suji kheer, boiled rice, etc. should be given to the patient.
ii. Proteins: Sufficient amount of proteins are required by the diarrhoea patient. Protein rich food like boiled eggs, toned milk etc. should be given to the patient with the improvement in his condition.
iii. Fats: Fats and fat rich foods are restricted to the diarrhoea patient because the intestine is incapable of absorbing them. Butter and light fats like cream can be given to the patient after the improvement in condition.
iv. Vitamins: Deficiency of water-soluble vitamins like vitamin B complex and C in the body is caused by the loss of water in diarrhoea. Hence, fruit juices must be added in the diet of the patient
v. Minerals: Loss of sodium and potassium leads to their deficiency diseases, like loss of appetite, vomiting, restlessness, loss of flexibility in

the muscles of the alimentary canal, etc. Their deficiency can be met by giving fruit juices to the patient after adding salt.

vi. Water: Patients should be given liquids in the form of mineral water, juices, soups, lemon water, barley water, etc. to overcome dehydration. Oral Rehydration Solution (ORS) should be given to prevent dehydration.

16. A day's menu for diarrhoea patient

- **Breakfast (8:00-8:30 AM):**
  - Vegetable soup (1 cup)
- **Mid-Meal (11:00-11:30 AM):**
  - Tender coconut water (1 cup)
  - 1 Apple (unskinned)
- **Lunch (2:00-2:30 PM):**
  - Khichdi (1/2 cup)
- **Evening (4:00-4:30 PM):**
  - Boiled black grams (1/3 cup)
  - Black tea (1 cup)
- **Dinner (8:00-8:30 PM):**
  - Khichdi (1/2 cup)

17. What are the points to be considered while planning meals for a diarrhoea patient?

- Small amount of food should be given to patient at regular intervals.
- In the beginning, food should be served at an interval of one and a half to two hours
- Avoid use of extremely hot and cold food

- Food should be simple and without spices
- Fibrous food should be avoided in diet
- Fried food should be avoided in diet
- More liquids should be given

18. Specify the nutritional requirements of a fever patient.

- Energy: An intake of 2500-3000 calories per day is recommended.
- Protein: Protein is very important to replace worn out cells by new cells and tissues. Hence, there is the requirement of more proteins
- Minerals: Calcium is very important for healing up of wounds in tuberculosis; this demand of calcium can be met by taking one litre of milk daily. Intake of iron should be increased if there is blood in sputum
- Vitamins: In the case of tuberculosis carotene is not converted into vitamin 'A' in the body. Therefore food containing more vitamin A and less carotene should be included in diet. Requirement of vitamin C is also increased. Vitamin D is important for the absorption of calcium. Requirement of vitamin B complex rises in proportion to the requirement of calories.

19. What are the causes of obesity

i. **Genetic factors**: Several studies show that there is a high correlation between obesity in parents and their children.
ii. **Physiological factors**: Men are more prone to subcutaneous fat deposition in the central part of chest and abdomen, while women show a greater proportion of fat at peripheral sites i.e., hip and thighs.
iii. **Dietary factors**: Dietary factors particularly the levels of fat and energy intake are strongly and positively associated with excess body weight.
iv. **Physical activity**: Reduced energy expenditure in adults has been shown to correlate with subsequent weight gain.
v. **Psychological factors**: Obese people seem to be affected more by taste and appearance of food rather than hunger and satiety. Tension, anxiety, fear and even humiliation associated with being obese, may further make a person resort to food for emotional satisfaction.

20. Explain the nutritional requirements for obese condition

i. **Energy**: The level of energy intake is adjusted to meet individual weight reduction requirements. A reduction of 500 kcal daily brings about a weight loss of 0.5 kg/week.
ii. **Protein**: It is advisable to give slightly higher than normal protein as it gives a feeling of satiety and also helps to maintain BMR. Include good quality proteins in the form of low fat milk and milk products, lean meats, egg white, whole pulses and whole cereals.
iii. **Fat**: 15-20% of total energy should be provided by fats.
iv. **Carbohydrates**: 60-65% of total calories should be provided by carbohydrates. Sugar should be limited. Dietary fibre provides bulk and satiety.
v. **Minerals and vitamins**: Fruits and vegetables should be amply included in the meals, as they are low in energy, a good source of vitamins and minerals and provide roughage which helps to relieve constipation.
vi. **Water**: Water is a key part of any weight loss programme. It is very necessary for helping the body remove fat and for general overall health.

21. Elaborate the dietary management of anaemia

i. The diet should be predominantly alkaline. The emphasis should be on raw fruits and vegetables, which are rich in iron. Iron rich vegetables are spinach, onions, carrots, radishes, beet roots, celery, yams, tomatoes and potatoes (with jackets).
ii. Fruits rich in iron include bananas, apples, dark grape, apricots, plums, raisins and strawberries. Bananas are particularly beneficial as they contain folic acid and vitamin B12 both of which are extremely useful in the treatment of anaemia.
iii. Other iron-rich food items are whole wheat, brown rice, beans, soyabeans, sunflower seeds, molasses, eggs and honey. Honey is also rich in copper, which helps in iron absorption. The diet should also be adequate in proteins of high biological value such as milk, homemade cottage cheese and eggs.
iv. Vitamin B12 is a must for preventing or curing anaemia. This vitamin is usually found in animal protein and especially in organic meats like kidney and liver. Other equally good sources of vitamin B12 are the various dairy products like: milk, eggs and cheese.
v. A liberal intake of ascorbic acid is necessary to facilitate absorption of iron. At least two servings of citrus fruits and other ascorbic acid rich

food should be taken daily.

vi. Beet roots can also be incorporated in the diet, which are extremely important in curing anaemia. Beet root juice contains potassium, phosphorus, calcium, sulphur, iodine, iron, copper, carbohydrates, protein, fat and vitamins like B2, B6, C, P and niacin. With its high iron content beetroot juice regenerates and reactivates the red blood cells and supplies the body with fresh oxygen.

CHAPTER V

Food Preservation

1 Mark Questions and Answers

1. Identify the odd one:

Dehydration (b) Smoking (c) **Refrigeration** (d) Sun drying

2. The mycotoxin produced by Aspergillus species of fungi called....... **(Aflatoxin)**

3. Identify the bacteriostatic method from the following:

Dehydration (b) Canning (c) **Pasteurization** (d) Boiling

4. Acid used to inhibit the growth of moulds in preserving jams and jellies

Benzoic acid (b) Lactic acid (c) Acetic acid

5. Find the odd one:

Citric acid (b) Sodium benzoate (c) Calcium propionate (d) Potassium meta bi sulphate

6. .... is the name given to the method employing temperatures below 100°C for the preservation of food.

Canning (b) Cellar Storage (c) Refrigeration (d) **Pasteurization**

7. .... is the name given to the method employing temperatures above 100°C for the preservation of food.

Canning (b) Cellar Storage (c) Refrigeration (d) Pasteurization

8. Name any two chemical preservatives used for food preservation **(Potassium metabisulphate, sorbic acid, calcium propionate and sodium benzoate)**

9. If pasteurization below 100^0C canning............. **(Above 100^0C)**

10. The optimum temperature of enzyme reaction is ....

37^0C (b) 40^0C (c) 53^0C (d) 5^0C

11. Odd one out:

(a) Fermentation (b) Germination (c) **Pasteurization** (d) Fortification

12. Class I preservatives: .... **(salt, sugars, oils, spices and condiments, vinegar and honey)**

Class II preservatives: .... **(sulphur dioxide, sodium and potassium metabisulphites, salicylic acid, benzoic acid, sorbic acid)**

13. The process of treating and handling food to stop or slow down food spoilage, loss of quality, edibility or nutritional value and thus allow for

longer food storage is called _____.

Food spoilage (b) Decomposition (c) **Food preservation** (d) None of these

14. Find out bactericidal method from the following

(a) **Canning** (b) Smoking (c) Freeze drying (d) Sun drying

15. Identify the method in which the food is frozen and the water from the food is removed under vacuum.

(a) Cellar storage (b) Refrigeration (c) Freezing temperature (d) **Freeze drying**

• • •

Short answer Questions and Answers

1. Define food spoilage

Food spoilage refers to the deterioration of the physical and chemical properties of food by the influence of air, heat, light, moisture etc. which foster the growth of microorganisms, making it unfit for consumption.

2. Discuss the classification of preservatives

PFA 1954 classifies preservatives into two types- Class I and Class II preservatives. Class I includes salt, sugars, oils, spices and condiments, vinegar and honey. Class II preservatives include sulphur dioxide, sodium and potassium metabisulphites, salicylic acid, benzoic acid, sorbic acid etc

3. Write the causes of Food Spoilage

1. **Improper handling**: It refers to workers who are not careful in transporting and handling the food resulting in cuts, bruises and blemishes. It also refers to the handling of food materials with dirty hands, in dirty containers and at dirty places.
2. **Improper storage**: Different food requires different places and temperatures for storage. For instance, fresh meat, fish and poultry are stored in cold storage and freezers. Fruits and vegetables are placed in airy and cool places or in the vegetable compartment of the refrigerator. Bulbs like onion, garlic and root crops are placed in baskets at room temperature.
3. **Inadequate preparation and cooking**: If foods like meat or fish is not prepared or cooked properly it will lead to spoilage.
4. **Careless packaging**: Packaging is important as it keeps bacteria and moisture away and maintains the quality of food. When meat, fish, fruits or vegetables are not properly wrapped before they are stored, it is easily

contaminated by microorganisms causing its spoilage.

4. Critically evaluate the role of microorganisms in causing food spoilage

Microorganisms that cause food spoilage are moulds, yeasts, bacteria Moulds- moulds are mainly found in decaying food. They contain spores which can spread through the air. Moulds cause vomiting. There are some yeasts termed as false yeast which is harmful to humans. They are found in pickles, jams etc Bacteria: Bacteria are unicellular organisms and are smaller in size than yeasts or moulds. They are more dangerous than yeast and moulds because they can spoil food without causing any change in the smell, appearance and taste. Bacteria generally prefer low acid foods like vegetables and meat. Eating food spoiled by bacteria results in food poisoning.

5. What do you mean by fermentation

The sugars present in the food are broken into alcohol and carbon dioxide. This process is called food fermentation.

6. What is the use of yeast in our daily life?

Yeasts are unicellular organisms coming under the kingdom fungi. They multiply very fast and cause fermentation on perishable food like fruit juices, syrups etc. Yeasts are beneficial agents used in various food preparations like appam, naan, bread etc. Fermentation is a desirable change brought about by the action of yeast, which results in the batter or dough to rise.

7. Discuss the effects of false yeast in our diet

False yeast which is harmful to humans. It grows as a dry film on the surface of very acidic and high sugar content food items such as pickle, jams etc. They survive at very low pH. During their growth, they produce certain metabolic end products that cause physical and chemical changes in foods resulting in food spoilage.

8. Write short notes on spoilage by enzymes.

When fresh food substances are kept at room temperature for a specific period of time, enzymes cause undesirable changes in colour, texture and flavour. These changes in food enable micro-organisms to contaminate the food leading to food spoilage.

9. Enlist the need for preserving food

- To add variety to the diet

- To make use of food when it is cheap and plentiful and to store it for later use
- To make the food available throughout the year.
- To retain as many of the qualities of the fresh food as possible such as flavour, texture, colour, appearance and nutritional value.
- To prevent micro organisms from contaminating the food once it is preserved, by sealing it from the outside air.

10. Define food preservation

food preservation can be defined as the process of treating and handling food to stop or slow down food spoilage, loss of quality, edibility or nutritional value and thus allow for longer food storage.

11. Differentiate bacteriostatic and bactericidal methods of food preservation

- **Bacteriostatic methods** Altering environmental conditions so as to prevent growth of microorganisms can help to preserve food. Such conditions are called bacteriostatic. eg: dehydration, pickling, salting, smoking, freezing etc.
- **Bactericidal methods** in which most of the microorganisms present in the food are killed, as in canning, cooking, irradiation etc

12. Differentiate cellar storage and refrigeration

- **Cellar storage (about 15°C):** Temperatures in cellars (underground rooms) where surplus food is stored in many villages are usually not much below that of the outside air and is seldom lower than 15°C. The temperature is not low enough to prevent the action of many spoilage organisms or of the plant enzymes. Eg. root crops, potatoes, onions etc. are stored for a limited period during the winter months.
- **Refrigeration or chilling temperatures (0°C to 5°C):** Chilling temperatures maintained by means of ice or mechanical refrigeration. Fruits and vegetables, meats, poultry, fresh milk and milk products etc. can be preserved from two days to a week when held at this temperature.

13. Write short note on freeze drying

In this method, the food is frozen and the water from the food is removed under vacuum. The water is converted into water vapour without passing through the liquid stage. The food is preserved in its natural state without any loss of texture or flavour. Food preserved using this method can be stored at room temperature. eg. Instant coffee, prawns, green peas etc.

6 Marks Questions and Answers

14. Explain the Bacteriostatic methods of food preservation

- **Dehydration (removal of water):** When the moisture in the food is removed and the concentration of water is brought below a certain level, they are unable to grow and spoil the food. Moisture can be removed by the application of heat as in sundrying and in mechanical heating or by binding the moisture with the addition of sugar or salt and making it unavailable to the microorganisms.
- **Sundrying**: Direct rays of the sun are used for drying a variety of food. Fruits, vegetables, cereals, pulses etc. are dried and stored in this method.
- **Smoking**: Food can also be dried by exposing them to smoke by burning some special kind of wood. In this method, while the heat from the smoke helps in the removal of moisture and exposure to smoke imparts a characteristic flavour to the food, eg. meat and fish.
- **Addition of salt and sugar**: Tying up moisture by addition of solutes such as salt or sugar also prevents growth of microorganisms and helps to preserve foods. The high concentration of sugar and other salts binds the moisture making it unavailable for micro-organisms to grow.
- **Use of oils and spices**: A layer of oil on the top of any food prevents the growth of microorganisms like moulds and yeasts. Thus, certain pickles in which enough oil is added to form a layer at the top can be preserved for long periods. Spices like turmeric, pepper and asafoetida have little bacteriostatic effect.
- **Use of acids**: Acidic conditions inhibit the growth of microorganisms. Organic acids are added or allowed in the food to preserve them. Acetic acid (vinegar), citric acid (lemon) and lactic acids are the commonly used preservatives.
- **Use of chemical preservatives**: Certain chemicals when added in small quantities can hinder undesirable chemical reaction in food.

15. Explain different bactericidal methods of food preservation (Killing)

i. Temperature below 100^0C (Pasteurization)

- **Pasteurization** is the name given to the method employing temperatures below 100°C for the preservation of food. Pasteurization is used widely in the treatment of milk. Here the milk is heated to 72°C or higher and kept at that temperature for at least 15 seconds. After pasteurisation, the milk is rapidly cooled to 10°C or lower and held at that temperature. This temperature inhibits the growth of microorganisms that may have survived. Fruit juices, aerated drinks are also preserved by this method.

ii. Temperature of boiling water 100°C

- **Boiling** - Cooking of rice, vegetables, meat etc. at home is usually done by boiling the food with water and involves a temperature around 100°C. Boiling the food at 100°C kills all the vegetative cells and spores of yeasts and moulds. Many foods can be preserved by boiling at home eg. milk.

iii. **Temperature above 100^0 C (canning)**

- **Canning** is one of the preservation methods in which processed food is sealed in an airtight container and heated above 100^0C to destroy microorganisms that can cause food spoilage. Canned food usually remains edible for one to five years. Canning retains maximum nutrients with minimal changes in appearance, taste and flavour. Fruits, vegetables, meat and meat products, fish and sausages are some of the commonly canned foods. Canned food ensures that the food substances are available throughout the year.

CHAPTER VI

Introduction to Fibre Science

1 Mark Questions and Answers

1. Which of the following is a synthetic fibre?

(a) Wool (b) Silk (c) **Polyester** (d) Cotton

2. The fibre obtained from the flax plant is:

(a) Jute (b) Hemp (c) **Linen** (d) Ramie

3. Which fibre is known for its elasticity and is often used in swimwear?

(a) Acrylic (b) **Spandex** (c) Nylon (d) Rayon

4. What is the main component of natural silk fibre?

(a) Cellulose (b) **Protein** (c) Polyester (d) Acetate

5. Which of the following fibres is most resistant to fire?

(a) Nylon (b) **Wool** (c) Cotton (d) Acrylic

6. Which of the following is a protein-based natural fibre?

(a) Cotton (b) **Silk** (c) Linen (d) Rayon

7. .... is known as Queen of Fibre

Cotton (b) Linen (c) **Silk (d)** Rayon

8. Choose the correct statement

(a) Wool is obtained hair of sheep (b) Silk is obtained from hair of silk worm

(c) Linen and jute obtained from leaves of plants (d) 4. Cotton is obtained from stem of plant

9. Identify the Fibre which is suitable for summer season.

(a) **Cotton** (b) Silk (c) Polyester (d) Nylon

10. Which natural fibre is known for its ability to 'breathe'?

(a) Polyester (b) Nylon (c) **Cotton** (d) Acrylic

11. .... are the fundamental visible units used in the fabrication of textile fabrics. **(Fibres)**

12. Give the odour of wool while burning (**hair burning smell)**

13. Give the odour of cotton while burning (**Paper burning smell)**

14. Give the odour of rayon while burning (**Paper burning smell)**

15. First manmade fibre .... **(Nylon)**

16. Gum present in the silk fibre is .... **(Sericin)**

17. Wool is Composed of a protein known as .... **(Keratin)**

• • •

Short Answer Questions and Answers

1. Illustrate the classification of textile Fibres

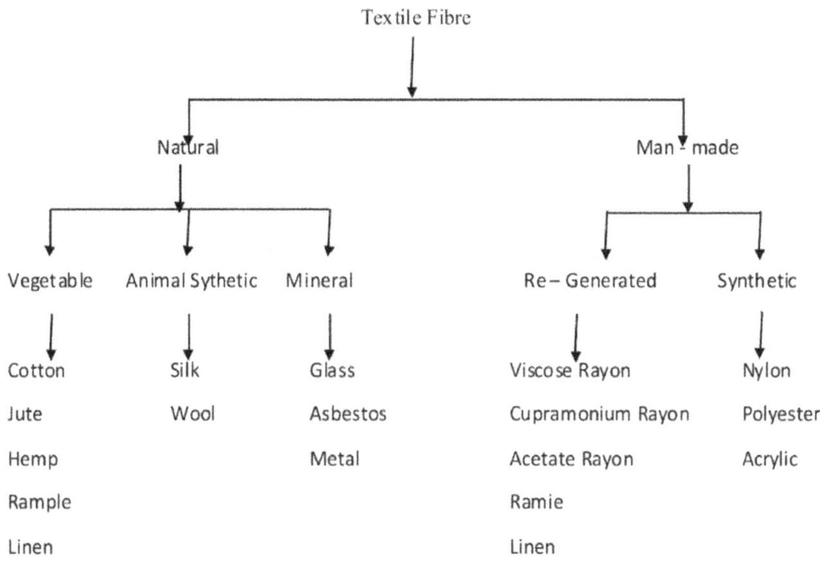

Classification of Textile Fibres

2. Explain the classification of textile Fibres according to their length

- **Filament Fibres**: These are natural or man-made Fibres of continuous length, measurable in yards or meters. Example: Silk and other man-made Fibres.
- **Staple Fibres**: Staple Fibres are short and measurable in inches and range from three quarters of an inch to eighteen inches in length. Example: All natural Fibres except silk.

3. Differentiate monofilament and multifilament fibres

- Monofilament Fibres: These are made up of single, smooth, solid strands. These are very strong and soft, so these are used in hosiery goods.
- Multifilament Fibres: These are composed of a number of tiny filaments twisted together. The size and number of filaments vary widely. These

are used for manufacturing lustrous and soft clothes.

4. Why cotton fabrics are suitable for summer

Cotton is a good conductor of heat. And mostly cotton Fibres have 8.5% of moisture but they have the ability to absorb 15- 20% of moisture. Due to this property they take time for drying. This is a positive property for cotton fabrics because they can absorb perspiration easily and give the feeling of coolness. That is why cotton is good for summers.

5. Why wool is used as a winter wear?

Wool is a bad conductor of heat. The scales on the surface of the wool and crimp in the Fibre create little pockets of air that serve as insulative barriers (bad conductor) and give warmth (Body heat is not radiating out and that is why it keeps the body warm).

6. Acrylic fibre acts as a substitute for wool in winter apparel. Give reason.

Acrylic fibre has excellent resistance to clothe moths, carpet beetles, mildew, bacteria and fungi. This is one reason why it is acting as a substitute for wool in winter apparel.

7. Polyester is not suitable for summer. Give reason.

Polyester is a bad conductor of heat. So body heat is not removed.Due to this it is not suitable for summer. Polyester does not absorb sweat. So it sticks to body. Due to this it is not suitable for summer.

8. Linen is suitable for summer season. Justify.

The fabric is a good conductor of heat and suitable for summers. Linen fabrics allow the body heat to go out and are comfortable during summers.

9. Silk is not suitable for summer season. Justify.

Silk fibre is a bad conductor of heat. The fabrics do not allow the body's heat to go out and are not suitable for summers.

10. Burning Test for the identification of Fibres

Fiber	Approach flame	Inflame	Odour	Ash/residue
Cotton	Ignites readily	Burns Quickly	Paper Burning	Soft grey
Wool	Melts Away	Burns Slowly	Hair Burning	Dark ash
Silk	Melts Away	Burns Slowly	Hair Burning	Dark ash
Rayon	Ignites readily	Burns Quickly	Paper Burning	Soft grey
Acetate	Fuses away	Burns Quickly	Paper Burning	Soft grey
Polyester	Shrinks away	Burns Slowly	Slightly Sweetish	Hard Brittle
Nylon	Shrinks away	Burns Slowly	Acrid line vinegar	Hard Brittle
Acrylic	Fuses & shrinks	Burns Quickly	Meat Burning	Hard Brittle

Identification of different fibres based on Burning test

11. Microscopic appearence of different textile fibres

1. Cotton

- Flat Fibre
- Ribbon like twist
- No crimp
- Central lumen
- No lustre

2. Silk

- Rod like structure
- Circular
- High lustre
- Gum present on surface
- No crimp

3. Wool

- Rough surface
- Crimp very evident
- Scales present

- More or less circular
- Lack of lustre

4. Nylon / Polyester

- Round rod like structure
- Smooth surface
- Translucent
- High lustre
- No crimp

6 Marks Questions and Answers

12. Explain the classification of textile fibres based on origin

i. **Natural Fibres:** Natural Fibres are Fibres that occur in nature.Natural Fibre can be of three types namely:

1. Vegetable Fibres: Vegetable Fibres are obtained from plants. The basic material of all plant life is cellulose.

- Example: - Cotton and kapok seed hairs.
- - Linen, jute and hemp are obtained from stems of plants.
- - Abaca and sisal are obtained from leaves of plants

2. Animal Fibres: Animal Fibres are obtained from animals. They are made up of proteins. Example: Wool -Hair of sheep, goat, rabbit or camel. Silk- Secretion of an insect (silk worm).

3. Mineral Fibres: are obtained from minerals. These are inorganic materials shaped into Fibres and are mainly used in fire proof fabrics. Example is asbestos.

ii. Man-made Fibres: All man-made Fibres are first made into filaments from which the fabric is woven. These are of two types. They are as follows:

1. **Synthetic Fibres:** These Fibres are obtained by a series of chemical reactions. Examples are Nylon, Polyester, and Acrylic etc.
2. **Regenerated Fibres:** The raw materials are from natural sources i.e. cellulose or protein. The properties of Fibre depend on the method of its manufacture and the source of the regenerated Fibres. Examples are

Rayon and cellulose acetate.

13. Comparison of physical properties of various textile fibres obtained from nature

Name of Fibre	COTTON *King of Fibres*	Linen Hygienic fibre	Silk 'Queen of Fibres'	Wool First Fibre that was used by primitive people.
Composition	Composed of 88-90% cellulose, 5-8% of water and natural impurities.	Composed of 66-70% cellulose and natural impurities	Fibre has a gum known as **sericin**.	Composed of a protein known as "**Keratin**".
Microscopic Structure	It appears as a narrow, flattened structure with spiral twists.	Fibre is shiny, flat and translucent. Nodes are present on the Fibre just like bamboo	The longitudinal section appears to be flat, uneven and ribbon like.	Cells are irregular in shape and slightly overlapping like scales of the fish. These are termed as **Serrations.**
Length	1/2"-2.5".	12 inches to 36 inches.	800-1300 yards.	2"-15".
Strength	Cotton Fibres are very strong. The strength increases on wetting up to 25% than when it is dry.	Linen is a very strong Fibre. It is stronger than cotton.	Silk is a strong Fibre.	It is stronger than silk. When wet, wool loses about 25% of the strength.
Moisture and absorption	They have the ability to absorb 15- 20% of moisture.	Linen absorbs more moisture than cotton.	Silk absorbs 10-30% of the moisture.	It has very high moisture absorption. It can absorb 30% moisture
Shrinkage	Cotton fabrics shrinks	Linen Fibre does not shrink like cotton.	Silk fabrics do not shrink after	Woolen Fibre has the ability to shrink

Physical Properties

Resiliency	Cotton fabrics have low resiliency and wrinkle easily unless they are given the finishing.	The Fibre wrinkles very soon just like cotton.	Silk is a resilient Fibre. Hence the wrinkles can be easily removed as compared to cotton.	Wool is highly resilient and comes to its original shape.
Effect of friction	It is not affected by friction.		Silk is a delicate Fibre which is affected by friction. Friction spoils the lustre and the texture of the Fibre.	
Effect of sunlight	Sunlight bleaches white fabrics. Coloured fabrics fade away if kept for longer duration.	Sunlight does not have any harmful effect on white fabrics.		Sunlight is not good for woollens but it can be kept in sunlight for shorter duration.
Heat conductivity	*Cotton is a good conductor of heat because it allows the body's heat to radiate out and keep body temperature stable i.e. normal temperature.*	The fabric is a good conductor of heat and suitable for summers.	This Fibre is a bad conductor of heat. The fabrics do not allow the body's heat to go out.	Wool is a bad conductor of heat.

Physical Properties of Textile Fibres

13. Comparison of chemical properties of various natural textile fibres

Fibre	Cotton	Linen	Silk	Wool
Action of acids	Strong acids destroy the Fibres but dilute acids have little or no effect.	Concentrated acids dissolve the Fibre. Dilute acids do not have any harmful effect.	Silks are damaged by concentrated acids. Acetic acid is used in the last rinse to restore Lustre of the silk.	Cold and Dilute acids do not harm the fabric. However, concentrated acids can destroy the Fibre.
Action of alkalis	Alkaline substances like borax, ammonia and caustic soda are not harmful for cotton. Strong alkalies change the nature of the Fibre.	Linen is not affected by alkalis.	Silk fabrics are damaged with alkalis. Strong alkalis weaken the fabric but weak alkalis like Borox and Ammonia can be safely used.	Concentrated alkalis destroy the Fibre immediately. Dilute alkalis and alkaline soaps also weaken the Fibre
Action of bleaches	All bleaching agents can be safely used on white cottons.	Different types of bleaches can be used on the fabric.	Sunlight and Chlorine damage the fabric.	Strong Bleaching agents are harmful to woollens.
Affinity for dyes	Cotton can easily be dyed with basic dyes. Salt is used to fix the dye on the fabric.	The affinity of the Fibres for dyes is less than that of cotton.	strong affinity to dyes. It can be easily dyed with acid, basic and direct dyes.	Wool has high affinity for most of the dyes especially Acid and Basic Dyes.

Chemical Properties of various textile fibres

14. Compare the effect of moth and mildew on various fibres

Effect of moth and mildew	Cotton is resistant to moth. Mildew and silverfish destroy the fabric. Fungal growth will occur during rainy season.	Linen is not susceptible to moth but develop mildew during rainy season.	Silk is not harmed by moth and mildew like wool.	Wool is easily damaged by moths. However, mildew does not easily attack except when stored in a damp place.

Effect of moth and mildew on various textile fibres

15. Compare the physical properties of any two manmade fibres

Name of Fibre	***NYLON*** *Nylon is the first man-made fibre*	**RAYON** Artificial Silk Regenerated manmade fibre.
Composition	Adipic acid and Hexamethylenediamine.	Cellulose as the main content along with carbon, hydrogen and nitrogen.
Microscopic Structure	nylon appears to be smooth, shiny and transparent. Tubular or round in cross section.	The microscopic structure of rayon is smooth, shiny and flat in appearance.
Length	It is a long filament which may be cut into staple length as required.	It is a long filament which may be cut into staple length as required.
Strength	This is the strongest among all the Fibres.	As compared to cotton, rayon is a weak fibre. In wet state the strength decreases.
Moisture absorption	It is a hydrophobic fibre which does not absorb moisture.	It absorbs water and is good for summer.
Shrinkage	Nylon does not shrink.	Rayon shrinks after washing and shrinkage is more than cotton.
Resiliency	Resiliency is good. Thus, nylon fabric does not crease easily and require less ironing.	Rayon is more resilient than cotton.
Effect of friction	It is a strong fibre and does not need precaution while washing. So friction can be used very easily on nylon fibre.	It cannot withstand friction and rubbing is harmful.
Effect of sunlight	Nylon does not have any effect of sunlight.	Does not have any harmful effects.
Heat conductivity	It is a bad conductor of heat	It is a good conductor of heat.

16.

Name of the Fibre	Obtained from	Also Known as
Cotton	Cotton Seed hair	King of Fibre
Silk	Silk worm	Queen of fibre
Linen	Stem of flax plant	Hygienic fibre
Wool	Hair of sheep	First used fibre
Rayon	Wood pulp	Artificial silk
Nylon	Adipic acid and Hexamethylene Diamine	First manmade fibre
Polyester	Polymer	Dacron or Terylene
Acrylic	acrylonitrile	Orlon or Cashmilon

CHAPTER VII

Yarn Production and Properties

1 Mark Questions and Answers

1. The process of twisting fibres together to produce yarn is called:

(a) Weaving (b) Knitting (c) **Spinning** (d) Plying

2. The term 'ply' in textiles refers to:

(a) The number of layers in a fabric (b) The thickness of a yarn (c) **The number of threads twisted together to make a yarn** (d) The pattern made by interlacing yarns

3. Pick the odd one

(a) Rotor spinning (b) Mechanical spinning (c) Friction spinning (d) **Fasciatedyarns**

4. Types of yarns are

(a) Single yarn (b) Ply yarn (c) _______ **(Cord yarn)**

5. The short length man-made yarns are called:

(a) Complex (b) Filament (c) **Spun** (d) None of these

6. Find the odd one:

(a) spun yarn (b) Tape yarn (c) Cord yarn (d) **Filament yarn**

7. Name any two non -conventional spinning methods (**Rotor spinning, friction spinning**)

8. .... is the oldest, most complex and also the most expensive method of manmade yarn manufacture. (**Wet spinning**)

Short Answer Questions and Answers

1. Define yarns

A yarn is a long continuous length of interlocked fibres. Strands of fibres are brought closer to each other by twisting. Twists impart strength to the fibre strand which is then termed as a yarn.

2. Write short notes on Spun yarns

- These are made by a number of staple (short) fibres twisted together.
- Natural fibres such as cotton, linen, wool and jute can be made into spun yarns.
- Even manufactured fibres can be cut into staple lengths and processed to give spun yarns.

- Spun yarn has a dull, fuzzy look. They are comfortable to wear and have less static build up.
- They soil readily and are prone to pilling.

3. What do you mean by tape, network or film yarns

- These are produced by splitting of sheets of materials which are extruded and solidified.
- One or more strips are made by lengthwise division of the polymer sheet.
- These yarns are cost effective and used in industrial textiles for packaging.

4. Explain the classification of yarns based on the function

1. **Simple yarns**: Simple yarns have a uniform size, regular surface and relatively smooth appearance. They have an equal number of twists per inch through their length. They are durable and helps prevent snagging and tearing. Such yarns are relatively easy to maintain.
2. **Complex yarns**: Fancy yarns bring an unusual look, variation and interesting effects into the fabric. Such yarns do not have a uniform thickness throughout their length. This in turn implies that they may show uneven performance in strength and wear.

5. Define Spinning

Spinning refers to the act or process of converting staple or short lengths of fibre (such as cotton or rayon) into continuous yarn or thread. It involves twisting the fibres together to create a cohesive strand that can be used for weaving or knitting fabrics

6. Explain the classification of yarns based on the number of constituent parts

1. **Single yarn**: It is made up of filament or staple fibres. Single yarns are rarely employed in textile applications. When the amount of twist is increased, it results in interesting effects eg. Crepe yarns.
2. **Ply yarn**: When two or more single yarns twisted together it results in ply yarns. Ply yarns are named on the basis of the number of single yarns used to make them. For example, 3 ply and 4 ply. Ply yarns are less

flexible, more coarse and heavier than single yarns.

3. **Cord yarns**: A cord yarn is composed of two or more ply yarns. For naming cord yarns, the number of plies as well as the number of single yarns in those plies is used. For example, 3, 2 ply cord yarn represents the use of 3 plies in yarn construction, each composed of 2 single yarns.

7. Explain the different types of chemical spinning

- **Melt Spinning** - The polymer is heated and melts to form a liquid spinning solution. eg.: Nylon, polymer etc.
- **Dry Spinning** – A volatile solvent (acetone) is used to dissolve raw materials and form a solution. eg.: Acetate.
- **Wet Spinning** - A non-volatile solvent is used to convert the raw material into a solution. eg: Viscose.
- **Gel-Spinning** - Polymer is mixed with a solvent to form a gel. This is passed through the same equipment as for melt spinning. The solvent is then extracted and the fibres are drawn.
- **Emulsion Spinning** - In this the polymer is made into an emulsion, forced through a narrow tube to align it, and then fused without melting by application of heat. This is followed by extrusion into a coagulating bath through a spinnerette and subsequently stretched to impart orientation

8. Explain the steps in chemical spinning

a. **Pre- Spinning Operations** - These include addition of delustrants (for reducing the bright lustre of manufactured fibres) to manufactured fibres.
b. **Actual Spinning** – This includes 3 steps. They are. Conversion of a polymer into a liquid or spinning solution, also called a dope followed by extruding the solution through spinnerets ie, pumping the dope. And solidification of the liquid into filaments (solids).
c. **Post-spinning operations** - These are common to all methods of chemical spinning and include washing, drawing (i.e., stretching) to improve orientation and heat setting

9. Describe the methods of spun yarn production

1. **Conventional/Mechanical Spinning** - This has been a commonly practised method of yarn production. Here, the fibres are made to pass through a series of machines that eventually convert them into yarn.
2. **Non Conventional** - Spinning Apart from the conventional ring spinning process, there are some non conventional processes as well. These include, Rotor spinning (Open end Spinning), Friction Spinning, Integrated Composite Spinning etc
3. **From manufactured filaments** - Spun yarns can be composed of fibres that are relatively short and are not exceeding eight inches. These yarns can be made from natural and man made fibres that fit the length ranges described. Spun yarns exhibit a hairy or fuzzy appearance.

10. Differentiate rotor spinning and friction spinning

- In rotor spinning, the sliver is fed into a rotary beater. This device ensures that the fibres are beaten into a thin supply which enters a duct and gets deposited on the sides of the disc (rotor). Turning of the rotor introduces twist in the fibre strand through air currents.
- In friction spinning, it consists of two perforated drums of the same diameter, moving in the same direction. Carded fibres are transported by air current to the rip of the rollers. They become compressed and twisted due to friction between rollers and strong air suction through the perforations. The final yarn is pulled out from below the roller and wound on a package placed at the top of the drums.

11. Describe the properties of yarns

- **Yarn twist** - Fibres are given a twist to hold them together and impart strength to a yarn. One end of the fibre strand is held stationery while the other end is revolved. The fibre then assumes a spiral position around the yarn axis.
- **Yarn number** - This is an indicator of yarn thickness. This is quantitatively expressed as a number, hence the term yarn number. There are two systems which can be employed to denote yarn fineness. These are the direct and indirect systems. Direct yarn number system used for filaments, expresses fineness as mass per unit length of yarn. Indirect yarn number system uses length per unit mass of yarns as an indicator of fineness

12. Evaluate the three important aspects of yarn twist

1. **Amount of twist** - The unit of twist is twist per inch (tpi) of yarn length. Generally filaments need a twist of 3-6 tpi while staples require a higher tpi of 10-20. More twist is required for staple, fine yarns and warp yarns. Twist is also qualitatively termed as low, medium and high. Low twist yarns are soft, fluffy, warmer, have more surface texture but show less resistance to abrasion and wearing due to lower strength.
2. **Direction of twist** - The twist in the yarns may be put either to the right (S) or left (Z). Regular weaving yarns are usually in these 2 twists. S-Right hand and Clockwise Z-Left hand and Counter Clockwise
3. **Degree of balance** - The balance of fibre is determined by the proportion of warp and weft yarns. If the numbers of warp and weft yarns are the same in a square inch the fibre has a good balance.

CHAPTER VIII

Fabric Construction

1 Mark Questions and Answers

1. Identify the comb like device which is placed towards the front of the loom.

(a) **Reed** (b) Shuttle (c) Harness (d) None of these

2. What is the process of interlacing two sets of yarns at right angles to each other to form a fabric?

A) Knitting B) **Weaving** C) Spinning D) Felting

3. Which of the following is a Surface Figure Weave

Dobby (b) **Swivel** (c) Double weave (d) Leno weave

4. The two types of felts are wool felts and _____ **(Needle felts)**.

5. What is the machine used to make woven fabric?

(a) Sewing machine (b) Embroidery machine (c) **Loom** (d) Knitting machine

6. .... is used to create woven fabrics by interlacing warp and weft yarns. **(loom)**

7. .... is the oldest method of fabric construction.

(a) **Weaving** (b) felting (c) laminating (d) knitting

8. .... is a comb-like device placed towards the front of the loom. **(Reed)**

9. The process of converting fibres directly into fabric is:

(a) Weaving B) Spinning C) Knitting D) **Felting**

10. Sateen is a variation of .... weave **(Satin)**

11. Brocades and damask are .... type of weave

Satin weave (b) Twill weave (c) **Jacquard weave** (d) satin weave

12. Find the odd one and give reason: Spot, Swivel, Lappet, Dobby

Ans. **Dobby**. (All others are surface figure weaves)

13. Mention the variations of plain weave. **(Rib weave, basket weave)**

• • •

Short Answer Questions and Answers

1. Define weaving

Weaving is the process in which two sets of yarns interlace at right angles to each other in patterns which are basic or fancy.

2. Define Knitting

Knitting is defined as an interloping of one or more yarns to make a fabric. Knitted fabrics are made from interlocking loops, formed from one or more yarns.

3. Describe Pile weaves

These weaves have a soft projecting surface of fibres. One set of yarns, called ground warp and weft form the base fabric in plain or twill weave. An extra yarn forms floats which are then cut and brushed to form the pile. Terry pile is an example of uncut pile whereas velvet is an example of cut pile fabrics.

4. Differentiate warp and weft yarns

Warp Yarns:

- Direction: Warp yarns run vertically along the length of the fabric.
- Strength: These threads are stronger and tauter because they form the backbone of the fabric.
- Function: The warp provides the structural support for the fabric.
- Appearance: In a bolt of fabric, the warp threads are the white threads running parallel to the selvage or fabric edge.

Weft Yarns:

- Direction: Weft yarns run horizontally from left to right across the fabric.
- Function: Weft threads weave in and out of the warp threads, filling out the fabric and adding colour or pattern.
- Ease of Removal: Weft yarns can be easily pulled out from the woven fabric if necessary.
- Length: Weft yarns are shorter, equal to the width of the fabric.

5. Write short note on tufting

- A woven fabric acts as the base and a set of pile yarns are inserted into it to form tufts or loops on one side. These may be cut and brushed.
- Fibres generally used for the base include cotton, linen and jute.
- A latex coating is then given at the back to enhance the stability of the tufted structure.
- Example: warm lining materials, bedspreads, blankets, rugs and carpets.

6. Write a short note on felting

These are fabric structures made by the interlocking of scales present on wool fibres. Technically any animal fibre can be used for felt construction.

Definition:

- Felting involves interlocking wool fibres to create a dense, matted material.
- It works with protein-based fibres like sheep wool, alpaca, mohair, and yak.
- Unlike bonded fabrics, felts don't need adhesive substances.

Methods:

- Wet Felting: Involves water, agitation, and compression.
- Lay out wool roving, add water, and rub to create a felted piece.
- Needle Felting: Uses barbed needles to tangle and compact fibres.
- Create flat or 3D shapes by poking the wool with needles.

Applications:

- Felting produces fabric, sculptures, and accessories.
- Woven fabrics made of cotton or wool can also be felted, resulting in thicker, compact materials

7. Write short note on Bonded fabrics

Bonded fabrics are fibre mats held together by adhesives, fusing chemicals or thermal means.

- **Composition:**
    - Bonded fabric consists of **fibres** joined together to form a sheet.
    - Unlike traditional woven fabrics, it doesn't involve yarns.
- **Properties:**
    - Bonded fabrics are **weaker** and more prone to tearing.
    - However, they don't stretch or fray.

  - Commonly used for disposable products, such as wet wipes and surgical gowns.

- **Applications:**

  - Bonded fabric finds use in various sectors:

    1. Clothing
    2. Outdoor gear
    3. Upholstery
    4. Automotive industry
    5. Packaging
    6. Home Textiles

6 Marks Questions and Answers

8. Explain the parts of a basic loom

1. **Warp Beam:**

   - Located at the back of the loom.
   - Holds the warp yarns (longitudinal threads).
   - Controlled to release warp yarns as needed during weaving

2. **Heald Shaft:**

   - Contains multiple wires, each with a hole or eye.
   - Threads the warp yarns.
   - Controls the production of the shed (the space between warp threads) using mechanisms like tappets, dobby or jacquard.

3. **Shuttle:**

   - Carries the weft yarn (horizontal thread) during weaving.
   - Completes the picking motion in shuttle looms.
   - Releases thread from a bobbin to form the filling cloth.

4. **Reed:**

- Consists of steel wire rods set vertically in a frame.
- Keeps warp threads evenly spaced.
- Feeds the filling thread into position by moving back and forth.
- Attaches the pick with the cloth's fell (edge)

5. **Cloth Roller:**
    - Located at the front of the loom.
    - Holds the produced fabric.
    - Fabric is wound on to this roller by the takeup motion.
6. **Picker:**
    - Attached to a spindle.
    - Receives motion from the picking arm.
    - Assists the shuttle in moving from one side to another
7. **Picking Stick or Arm:**
    - Wooden arm or stick that imparts motion to the picker.
8. **Temple:**
    - Supports maintaining a fixed width dimension at the cloth edges
9. **Lease Rod:**
    - Guides the warp yarns.
    - Two wooden or glass rods set between the whip rolls and heddles.
    - Keeps alternating warp threads separate

9. Explain the mechanism or motions in weaving
Shedding:

1. The shedding mechanism **separates the warp threads** into two layers or divisions, creating a tunnel known as the **"shed."**
2. The shed provides room for the passage of the shuttle.

Picking:

- Picking involves **propelling the weft yarn** through the open shed.
- Shuttle is used for picking.

Beat-up:

- After each weft insertion, the reed moves forward to **compact the weft yarn** against the fabric already woven.
- Achieves uniform fabric density and interlocking of weft and warp threads.

Primary motion		Secondary motion
Shedding	- Harness frame	Take up Cloth beam
Picking	- Shuttle	Let off Warp beam
Beating	- Reed	

10. What are the different types of looms

- **a) Source of power**: Based on the source of power, looms can be classified as handlooms and power-looms. Looms that are manually operated are referred to as handlooms. The power loom is run by mechanical energy. It is faster than a handloom.
- **b) Mechanism of laying the weft yarn**: Based on the mechanism of laying the weft yarn the looms can be classified as shuttle and shuttle-less looms. The loom that uses a shuttle for laying the pick is referred to as a shuttle loom. In shuttleless looms the pick is laid across the shed using a variety of mechanisms.

11. Describe any five characteristics of woven fabrics

1. **Warp or end:** it refers to the yarns laid lengthwise on the loom. Cross wise yarns are called weft, pick or filling yarns. Warp yarns are generally stronger than weft yarns.
2. **Bias:** It refers to a direction which is at 450 angles to the warp and weft. There is maximum stretch along the bias of a fabric.
3. **Fabric count (thread count):** It is an indicator of the compactness of a weave. It is defined as the number of warp and weft yarns per square inch of a woven fabric.
4. **Balance:** It is the ratio of the warps to wefts in one square inch. A balanced fabric is one in which this ratio is 1:1.
5. **Selvedge or selvage** is the 'self-edge' of a woven fabric. They are the two longer sides of the fabric, which have edges and that do not need any kind of finishing.

12. Explain basic weaves

There are three basic weaves from which all woven fabrics are constructed. These are plain weave, twill weave and satin weave.

Plain weave

- The plain weave is the simplest of the three basic weaves.
- The plain weave is formed by yarns at right angles passing alternately over and under each other.
- Plain weave requires only two- harness looms and the least expensive weave to produce.
- It is described as a 1/1 weave
- Examples of fabrics with plain weave are organdie, muslin, cambric, poplin, flannel and canvas.

Twill weave

- In twill weave the order of interlacing causes diagonal lines to appear in the fabric.
- The lines may run to the right, known as the Z direction, or they may run to the left, known as the S direction.
- The fabrics with twill weaves are attractive, durable and strong. Being tightly woven, they do not get as dirty as plain weaves
- Examples include denim, drill, some tweeds and many suiting fabrics

Satin weave

- A basic satin weave repeats over at least five 'ends' and five 'picks', but the warp 'ends' interlace only once.
- This type of weave pattern leads to the creation of long 'floats' which because of the scarcity of interlacings (and thread density)
- It produces the smooth, even and lustrous sheen often associated with satin.
- Satin weave fabrics less durable and weaker than plain or twill weave fabrics.
- Satins find wide use as lining fabric and in sarees.

13. Explain any four fancy weaves

Fancy weave refers to any weaving method other than plain, twill or satin weaves used to create a fabric with a surface texture or pattern resulting from the interlacing pattern.

Dobby weave

- Dobby weaves generally have unique geometric patterns in the fabric.
- Dobby fabrics can come in all kinds of patterns, colours, weights and hand feels.
- Examples include honey comb and birds' eye. It is not possible to remove the design without unravelling the fabric.

Jacquard weave

- This is one of the most elaborate weaves, made by evenly combining plain, twill and satin weaves in the same crosswise yarn.
- It is a fabric woven on a special loom called the **jacquard loom**
- Jacquard fabrics have floats and lustre.
- They are more stable and stretcher than the fabrics made through basic weaves.
- It has elaborate patterns and scenes that make it extremely attractive and also expensive.
- Examples include brocades and damask.

Leno weave

- This is characterised by an open mesh structure which is achieved through a doup attachment on the loom.
- This controls the warp yarns by moving vertically as well as horizontally.
- The weave is also sometimes referred to as doup weave.
- Fabrics produced with such crossed yarn arrangements exhibit superior strength, reduced shrinkage and slippage.

Double weaves

- These are made with 3, 4 or 5 sets of yarns.
- Double cloth which is made from 3 yarns is also called a double faced or backed fabric.
- There could be 2 sets of warp yarns, which share one filling yarn.
- Examples include satin ribbons, interlinings of coats and reversible blankets.

14. Briefly explain the different types ofSurface figure weaves

1. **Spot or dot weave:**

- A certain series of yarn either the warp or the filling inserted to the surface of the cloth at certain points and allowing it to float for a number of ends or picks as the case may be thus producing a spotted effect on the cloth.
- Spots may be made by floating either the warp or the filling on the face of the cloth.
- The 'eyelash' patterned fabric (dotted Swiss) is one example of clipped spot.

2. **Swivel weave:**

- Swivel weaves require an extra filling yarn to form the design.
- The same filling yarn is used to produce the entire motif.
- Cotton sarees from Calcutta are a common example of swivel weave.

3. **Lappet weave:**

- Extra warp yarn is used to create a pattern which is securely fastened to the ground weave.
- Fabrics with this weave are durable and expensive.
- The effect sometimes resembles hand embroidery or machine hakoba embroidery.

15. Compare and contrast knitting with weaving

- Knitting is 'younger' to weaving as a fabric construction process.
- Yardage as well as garments can be made on knitting machines while looms produce only yardage.
- Knitting is two to five times faster than weaving.
- Knitting involves formation of loops, thus a greater length of yarn is used up to form loops across the width and along the length of a knitted fabric.
- Knits have greater porosity but lesser cover than woven fabric.
- Fineness of construction is indicated by gauge or cut in knits, as against fabric count or thread count in woven fabric.
- Wide knitting machines run as fast as the narrow ones; in weaving wider looms have a slower speed of production.
- Yarn specifications for knitting are more stringent than for weaving. This escalates the cost of raw material. However, no yarn preparation like sizing, washing etc. is needed in knitting.

16. Compare Weft knitting and warp knitting

1. **Weft Knitting**:

    - Also known as "normal" knitting done at home.
    - Built in horizontal rows, increasing in length.
    - Formed by intermeshing loops from a single strand of yarn.
    - Common techniques include plain or garter knit, purl knit, knit-purl, and rib knit.
    - Used for tailored garments, hosiery, skirts, t-shirts and textured fabrics.

2. **Warp Knitting**:

    - Done on machines.

- ◦ Built by column, growing in width.
- ◦ Each loop made from a different strand of yarn in a horizontal direction.
- ◦ Requires as many needles and strands of yarn as there are "loops" across the width.
- ◦ Produces stable fabrics due to intermeshing of warp yarns

17. Briefly explain the fabric construction methods other than woven and non- woven.

Braided fabrics

- Braids are primarily a trimming fabric with three or more yarns interlaced diagonally.
- Braids are very strong in the lengthwise direction.
- In braiding, the yarns are not interlaced at right angles as in weaving, nor are they looped as in knitting. Rather the yarns are connected by twisting or by knotting them together. These can be used for trimmings or joined together to form a fabric.
- Used in craft items and bags made of jute or coir braids, shoelaces, wicks and electrical wire coverings.

Laces

- The starting material for lace is generally a thread and not a yarn.
- If however a yarn is used then it is given enough twist to strengthen it.
- Lace may be knotted, interlaced, twisted or knit.
- All laces are characterised by an open mesh structure and decorative design.
- Handmade lace is called real lace. Lace fabrics may now be constructed by a weaving technique on a complex piece of equipment called the leaver's machine.
- Lace fabrics can also be made up into dresses, curtains and table cloths.

Laminated fabrics

- Laminated fabrics is a layered fabric structure in which surface fabric is joined to a backing fabric with an adhesive.

Nets

- Nets are open work fabrics made by threads or yarns, on bobbinet machines in which the bobbin yarns are looped around the warp yarns in a spiral formation.
- This produces large geometric open gaps between yarns with no designs.
- Applications include veils, curtains, fishing nets, sports equipments and hammocks.

CHAPTER IX

Fabric Finishing

1 Mark questions and Answers

1. This process increase the luster and smoothness by burning the surface lightly.

(a) Bleaching (b) **Singeing** (c) Stiffening (d) Scouring

2. Name the finishing process which gives whiteness to the fabric.

(a) **Bleaching** (b) Scouring (c) Singeing (d) Calendaring

3. Which of the following is a classification of finish based on the function ?

(a) Temporary finishes (b) Permanent finishes (c) **Aesthetic finishes** (d) Mechanical finishes

4. What is the primary purpose of the mercerization process in textile manufacturing?

(a) To make the fabric waterproof (b) **To increase the fabric's strength and luster** (c) To make the fabric shrink-resistant (d) To dye the fabric more easily

5. Give two examples of permanent finishing **(Water proofing, fire proofing)**

6. Identify the fabric finishing which is also known as pre shrinkage **(Sanforization)**

7. Finishing which makes cotton fabrics transparent and stiff is known as...... **(Parchmentization)**

8. Finish given to remove the wrinkles in the fabric .... **(Calendering)**

9. Select the permanent finish from the following

(a) Starching (b) Bleaching (c) W**ater proofing** (d) Calendaring

10. Give another name of the following finishes

(a) Removal of starch: .... **(Desizing**) b) Improves whiteness: ... **(Bleaching)**

• • •

Short answer questions and Answers

1. How fabric finishes are classified based on the process involved

- **Mechanical finishes** - They involve specific physical treatments like application of moisture, pressure, heat etc. and are given to that fabric surface to cause a change in the fabric appearance. eg. beating, brushing, calendaring etc.
- **Chemical finishes** - These finishes are those in which a chemical reaction alters the chemical structure of the fabric. The appearance and the basic properties are changed permanently eg. fire proof, crease resistance.

2. Write the advantages of bleaching

- Bleaching gives whiteness to the fabric
- It helps in the easy dyeing and printing of the fabric
- Special finishes can easily be given to bleached fabric
- It enhances the quality, absorbency and lustre of the fabric
- The chemicals used in bleaching disinfect the fabric.

3. Differentiate Degumming and weighting

- Degumming of silk is the process of removing the sericin layer from raw silk fibres. Sericin is a non-filamentous protein that covers the silk threads and allows them to stick together.
- The weight of certain fabrics like silk is increased by giving this finish. After degumming the silk fabrics become soft and light. This loss of weight is compensated by treating silk with suitable organic and inorganic compounds such as salts of tin, aluminium, iron and tannin acid.

4. Define Parchmentization

Parchmentization is the process in which the cotton fabrics are treated with dilute sulphuric acid that result in a transparent and stiff fabric. This fabric is called organdie.

5. List out the advantages of parchmentization.

- This fabric is thin, transparent, light weight and stiff.
- They seem to be heavily starched but do not need starching.

6. Differentiate beetling and singeing

- **Beetling** - The fabric is beaten with large wooden blocks in order to produce a hard flat surface with sheen. This action closes the interstices of the weave, flattens the yarns and gives greater areas for reflection of light, this increases the fabric lustre.
- **Singeing** - Singe means to burn the surface lightly. The fabric passes over brushes to raise the fibres, and then passes over heated copper plates or flame at high speed. The surface fibres are burned. This process increases the lustre and smoothness of the fabric made from staple fibre.

7. Write notes on Mercerization. List the advantages of Mercerization

In this process the fabric is soaked for 15 minutes in 15-20% solution of caustic soda under regulated pressure and temperature. After this the fabric is washed and neutralized in dilute acidic solution. Then it is washed in water and dried.

Advantages

- The fabric becomes strong and durable.
- The fabric becomes more compact.
- Increases the glazeness and lustre of the fabric and gives a silk like appearance.
- Absorbency increases.
- Affinity for dyes increases and makes printing and dyeing easy.
- Dyed in fast colour.

8. What do you mean by sizing and de-sizing

- Finishing that gives stiffness to the fabric and helps in maintaining its shape is called sizing. Normally starches, dextrin, gelatine, oil and wax are used for sizing.
- De-sizing is the removal of this sizing or starch. Depending on the fibre that has been used the cloth may be steeped in a dilute acid and then rinsed or enzymes may be used to break down the size. Silk fibres undergo degumming since sericin gum imparts stiffening to silk fabrics.

9. Explain any two permanent methods of fabric finishing

- **Water proofing**: Finishing which does not allow the entry of water into the fabric is known as water proofing and the fabric is known as water proof fabric. A coating of rubber, oxidized oil, varnish, resin, silicon etc. are applied on the fabric for making such fabrics. The openings of the fabric are filled up and water slips over it.

- **Wrinkle-Free Finish**: Also called crease-resistant finish, it prevents fabric from wrinkling during use and washing

10. Enlist the importance of fabric finishing

1. **Improve the appearance** - Fabrics undergo finishing to improve their colour, pattern or sheen.
2. **Change the texture of the fabric** – Some finishes are used to make the fabrics smooth and shiny. The texture of the fabric can be changed by embossing, brushing or smoothing.
3. **Improve the feel** – Fabrics or fibre can be made softer, crisper, firmer etc., by the application of various finishes.
4. **Improve the drape** - The hanging quality of the fabric can be improved by applying finishes like weighting.
5. **Improve the wearing qualities** - Certain finishes like crease resistance, stain resistance, flammability, water proof etc., make the fabric suitable for the particular purpose for which they are meant.

11. Illustrate the Classification of fabric finishes

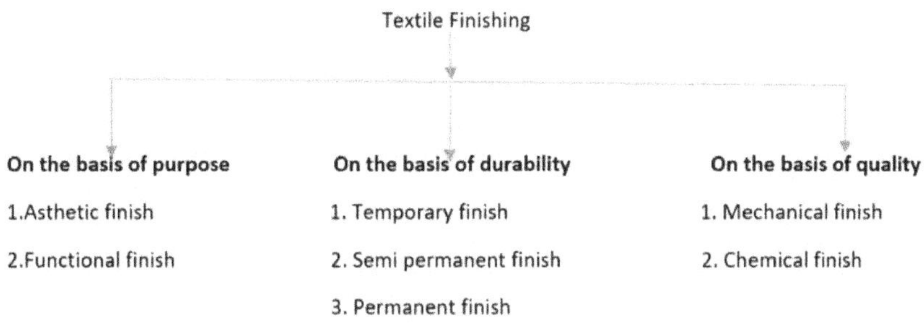

12. **Explain the classification of fabric finishes based on purpose or function**

- **Aesthetic finishes / basic finishes** - Aesthetic finishes improve the appearance and or hang or drape of the fabric eg. mercerization, stiffening, softening, calendaring etc.

- **Functional finishes/ Specific finishes** - Functional finishes or specific finishes change the properties of the fabrics. It also improves its performance for specific purposes eg. fire proofing, water proofing

13. Briefly explain the classification of fabric finishes based on durability

- **Temporary finishes** - These finishes got removed or diminished the first time the article is laundered or dry-cleaned. e.g. starching, softening and bleaching of white fabrics.
- **Semi durable finishes** - These finishes remain on the fabric for several washes and dry cleaning and it may be removed after several laundering: eg. bleaching.
- **Durable finishes** - These finishes last throughout the life of the fabric but its effectiveness diminishes after each washing and by the end of the life of the fabrics, the finish may disappear eg. shrinkage resistance.
- **Permanent finishes** - These finishes impart chemical change in the fibre structure and as a result they do not change throughout the life of the fabric, eg. Water proofing, fire proofing.

14. Write any three mechanical methods of fabric finishing

- **Calendaring**: The fabric is passed through a series of smooth hot rollers to remove wrinkles. It makes the fabric smooth and lustrous, thereby improves its appearance. The calendaring effect on the fabric is usually temporary and disappears after first washing.
- **Tendering**: The fabric becomes irregular in width after the process of weaving and washing. Tendering finish is given to a fabric to bring the fabric to normal width. Tendering machine is 20-90 ft in length and has hooks on both sides. Selvedges of the fabric are firmly fixed in hooks on both the ends. Steam is passed on the fabric and when the fabric regains normal width, it is passed through hot air chambers where it dries up.
- **Sanforization**: Sanforization is the method of stretching, shrinking and fixing the woven cloth in both length and width to reduce the shrinkage. The fabric is stretched and pressed against a hot roller which makes the surface of the fabric compact.

15. Explain any three chemical methods of fabric finishing

- **Scouring**: Scouring is the chemical washing process done on fabrics to remove natural wax, dirt or other impurities accumulated in the manufacturing process. This makes the fabric more smooth, neat and absorbent.
- **Parchmentization**: Parchmentization is the process in which the cotton fabrics are treated with dilute sulphuric acid that result in a transparent and stiff fabric. This fabric is called organdie.
- **Mercerization**: In this process the fabric is soaked for 15 minutes in 15-20% solution of caustic soda under regulated pressure and temperature. After this the fabric is washed and neutralized in dilute acidic solution. Then it is washed in water and dried. The fibre becomes more lustrous than the original fibre and its strength increases by 20%.

16. **Give the other name for the following processes**

- **Sanforization** - Pre- shrinkage
- **Singeing** - Burning the surface of the fabric
- **Increasing the weight** – weighting
- **Tendering** - Pulling the fabric by width
- **Desizing** - Removal of starch
- **Degumming** – Removal of sericin

Fabric Finishing methods

Mechanical (Dry finishing)– Beetling, singeing, tendering, calendaring, sanforization

Chemical (Wet finishing) – Weighting, degumming, bleaching, scouring, mercerization, parchmentization

Permanent finishes – fire proofing, water proofing, crease resistant

Temporary finishes – sizing, calendaring, starching

CHAPTER X

Dyeing and Printing

1 Mark Questions and Answers

1. Tie and dye is an example of......... dyeing (**Resist Dyeing**)
2. Roller printing is a machine counterpart of _____. (**Block printing**)
3. Choose the incorrect statement.

1. (a) Photographic and tonographic with multiple colours can be printed on textiles through digital printing.
2. (b) Screen printing was referred as silk screen printing.
3. (c) **Block printing is the new method of printing design on fabric.**
4. (d) Roller printing is the machine counter part of block printing.

4. _______ is a resist dyeing process where designs are made with wax on a fabric.

(a) Tie and dye (b) Block Printing (c) **Batik** (d) Roller Printing

5.Different stages of dyeing are given below. Find the missing one.

(a) Solution dyeing (b) Stock dyeing (c) Yarn dyeing (d) Product dyeing **(fabric dyeing)**

6. Find the odd one from the following:

(a) Block printing (b) **Discharge printing** (c) Stencil Printing (d)Roller printing

• • •

Short Answer Questions and Answers

1. Define dyeing

Dyeing is the irreversible application of colour on a textile substrate. In this process the fibre, yarn or fabric is impregnated with dye stuff.

2. Roller printing is a machine counterpart of block printing. Explain

Roller printing is a machine counterpart of block printing. Here designs are imprinted on the cloth by engraved copper cylinders or rollers. There are large numbers of engraved rollers as there are colours in the design to be imprinted. The rollers rotate in the print paste. The engraved patterns pick up the print paste and transport it to the fabric. Roller printing is a high - speed process which can produce up to 6000 yards of printed fabric in an hour.

3. What is Block printing?

Block printing is a hand method and the oldest method of printing design on fabric. To make hand blocked prints, the design must be carved on wooden or metal blocks first. The dye stuff is applied in paste form to the design on the face of the block. The block is pressed down firmly by hand on selected portions of the fabric.

4. Write a short note on Screen printing

Screen printing is also known as silk screen printing because the screens were made of fine, strong silk threads. Today they are also made of nylon, polyester, and metal. Screen printing can be used for the production of larger patterns. The colours can be produced in brighter, clear shades than with roller printing.

5. Write the advantages of digital printing

- Multiple shades as well as colours can be printed on textiles. Any number of colours can be printed in fabrics
- It offers faster processing speed where everything that is required in the print can be prepared on computer digitally
- Large quantities of printing can be done with less time
- It allows the user to print even smaller quantity. Therefore there is no minimum order quantity
- High Precision in printing is possible, which is usually a drawback with other forms of printing.
- Digital printing is cheaper compared to other printing methods.

6 Marks Questions and Answers

6. Classification of dyes

The dyes can be classified based on their chemical composition. They are:

1. Acid dyes / Anionic dyes

- Acid dyes require an acidic bath for their application.
- It is mostly used for protein fibres like wool and silk.
- Acid dyes or anionic dyes are inexpensive and fairly fast to light.
- They have low resistance to perspiration.
- These dyes are not suitable for cottons and other cellulose fibres as they harm the fibre.

2. Basic dyes / Cationic dyes

- Basic dyes are salts of carbon.
- Basic dyes are used with mordents for cottons, linen acetate, nylon, polyester, acrylics etc.
- When used with natural fibres, basic dyes are not fast to light, washing, perspiration or atmospheric gases.
- They give fastness and bright shades to acrylics for which they are mainly used.

3. Disperse dyes

- Disperse dyes are not soluble in water; they are supplied in finely ground form that will disperse in water.
- The particle will dissolve in the fibres and by this action, the fabric is dyed.
- They are mostly used for polyester, nylon and cellulose acetate.

4. Vat dyes

- They are insoluble pigments, but are made soluble in water by the use of strong reducing agents.
- They are the fastest dyes for cotton, linen and rayon.
- Vat dyes are used for fabrics that are washed regularly as they are fast and durable and can resist light, sweat, acid, alkali, washing etc.

5. Azoic dyes / Napthol dyes

- Azoic dyes are widely used on cellulose fibres.
- They are also referred to as 'ice colours' since their application sometimes involves the use of ice to lower the temperature and to assure efficient dye formation.
- Bright colours are produced at relatively low cost with the added advantage of colour fasteners to washing and light.

6. Direct dyes

- Direct dyes have a natural affinity to cellulose and can be applied without using a mordant.
- They can be dyed easily at a low cost, but the colours are not fast and durable.
- These colours cannot resist sunlight and washing.

7. Reactive dyes

- Reactive dyes are sometimes called fibre reactive dyes.
- They react with fibre molecules to form a chemical compound.
- Reactive dyes have excellent fastness to light and washing and they also give brilliant shades.

7. Explain the different stages of dyeing

Dye can be applied at any stage of production namely spinning fibre, yarn and fabric or during the garment stage. There are five stages of dyeing. They are:

1. Solution dyeing or dope dyeing

During the production of man-made, the dyes or pigment is added to the solution before it is extruded through the spinnerets into filaments. This process is called solution dyeing or dope dyeing. This method is also called mass pigmentation.

2. Stock dyeing / Fibre dyeing

Stock dyeing refers to dyeing a textile fibre in a loose condition before it is spun. This is done by putting it in large vats and circulating dye liquor through the mass of fibre at elevated temperature.

3. Yarn dyeing

When dyeing is done after the fibre has been spun into yarns, it is described as yarn dyeing. Yarn dyed fabrics are usually deeper and richer in colour. They provide adequate colour, absorption and penetration for most colours.

4. Fabric dyeing

Fabric dyeing is also known as piece dyeing. It is dyeing fabric, after it has been constructed. It is economical and the most common method of dyeing solid coloured fabrics.

5. Product dyeing

Product dyeing also known as garment dyeing, is the process of dyeing products such as hosiery, sweaters and carpet after they are produced.

8. Explain the basic styles or Principles of printing

There are five basic styles of printing. They are

Direct printing

- Direct printing is the oldest style of printing. In which the print paste is applied directly on the surface of the fabric. The dyes are usually dissolved in water to which a thickening agent has been added to give the necessary viscosity to the print paste. Example: Block printing

Resist printing

- In resist printing, certain portions of the fabric or yarn are resisted from taking up the print paste. The resisting agents may be physical or chemical in nature. It can be a thread, molten wax, mud, stencil, screen etc. Example: Tie and dye, Batik, Stencil printing and screen printing.

Discharge printing

- In discharge printing, discharge paste which contains chemicals to remove the colour is printed on the fabric. Sometimes, the base colour is removed and another colour is printed in its place, but usually a white area is desirable to brighten the overall design.

Mordant printing

- Mordants are chemical substances used in dyeing and printing with natural dyes. They have the capacity of combining with both the substrate and dye stuff thus forming a link between the two.

Transfer printing

- Transfer printing transfers thermoplastic ink designs from a roll of paper to the fabric. The design is first printed on to a flexible non textile substrate and later it is transferred to a fabric. The patterns are transferred by the application of heat and pressure. So this technique is sometimes referred to as heat – transfer printing.

9. Elaborate tie and dye as a resist dyeing method. What are the different tying methods used in tie and dyeing.

1. Tie and dye

The fabric or yarn to be dyed is folded and tied with strings or narrow strips of cloth. The strings or strips are waxed to increase the resistance and get better results. This prevents the dye from reaching some parts of the fabric, and restricts the amount absorbed on other parts so that a pattern is created. The skin of yarn or the fabric is then dipped in dye bath and dyed a number of times in different colours. It is then dried and the strings are removed. Only that portion of the fabric that is not tied will absorb the dye, as the string on the cloth serves as a resist.

Designs are created in tie and dye through the following processes

1. **Marbling:** Take the fabric and crumble it to form a ball. Tie it with a thread at different areas, randomly. Then dye the fabric. Open it and dry. The dyed fabric will have a marble effect.
2. **Binding:** Pick up the fabric from one point and tie with a thread at intervals and dye it.
3. **Knotting:** Put knots on the fabrics wherever desired and dye it.
4. **Folding:** Put the fabric flat on a table. Pleat and fold it uniformly in lengthwise direction. Tie it with yarn at regular intervals, to get width wise lines after dyeing. For horizontal lines, pleat and fold the fabric width wise. Roll or fold the fabric from one corner to the diagonally opposite corner and tie at regular intervals to get diagonal lines.
5. **Clump tying:** Take some beads or pebbles and put them in the fabric and then tie.

10. Explain any two methods of resist dyeing

Batik

- The fabric is stretched on a frame and hot melted wax is applied using a brush. When the wax is set, the fabric is piece dyed in cold water dye bath. After drying more wax is applied on the design and again piece dyed. Batik works best on absorbent fabrics such as silk or cotton. Synthetic fibres do not absorb the wax or dye readily.

Stencil printing

- In stencil printing, the design is first cut in card board, wood or metal. After positioning the stencil, colour is brushed or sprayed across the stencil cut. The die penetrates through the open area in the stencil. Colour can be applied with brushes, sponge, spray or toll to achieve various effects.

CHAPTER XI

Extension Education

1 Mark Questions and Answers

1. Choose the incorrect statement related to formal education

a. Authority rests with the teacher (c) Teaching is mainly rigid
b. Class attendance is compulsory (d) **It has no fixed curriculum**

2. Name an extension teaching method **(Individual method, Group method, Mass method)**

3. Fill the missing one

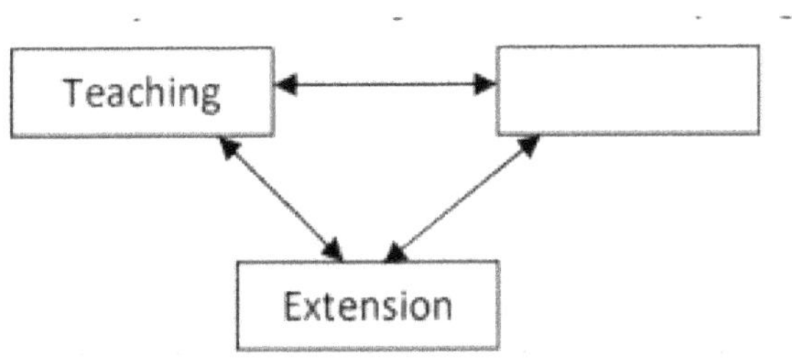

Research

4. An out-of school system of education is ________.

(a) **Extension education** (b) Formal education (c) Continuous education (d) None of these

5. Fill this.

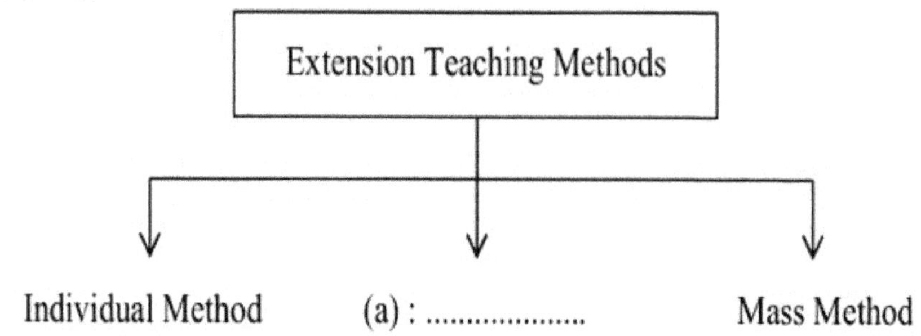

Group method

6. Extension education is:

Informal education (b) Formal education (c) **Non-formal education** (d) All of the above

7. The word "extension" is derived from:

(a) **Latin word** (b) Greek word (c) English word (d) None of the above

8. Extension education follows which communication process?

(a) **Two-way** (b) One-way (c) Both A and B (d) None of the above

9. The first step in the Extension Educational Process is:

(a) **Analysis of the situation** (b) Deciding on realistic objectives

(c) Evaluation (d) Re-consideration

• • •

Short Answer Questions and Answers

1. Define Home Science extension

According to Chandra, the term 'Home Science Extension' is "the dimension of social science which concerns itself with functional and attitudinal changes in the home and the family through scientific and technological knowledge.

2. Define Extension Education

The term **'Extension Education'** means that type of education which is 'stretched out' into villages and fields, beyond the limits of schools and colleges, where the formal type of education is normally confined. In other words the word 'Extension' used in this context signifies an **out of school system of education.**

6 Marks Questions and Answers

1. What are the objectives of extension education?

1. To assist people discover and analyse their problems, their felt needs and unfelt needs.
2. To develop leadership among people and help them in organizing groups to solve their problems.
3. To disseminate information based on research and /or practical experience, in such a manner that the people would accept it and put it into actual practice.
4. To keep the research workers informed of the people's problems from time to time, so that they may offer solutions based on necessary research.

2. Write the scope of extension education

- Extension is education for all village people.
- Extension is bringing about desirable changes in the knowledge, attitudes and skills of people.
- Extension is helping people to help themselves.
- Extension is working with men and women, boys and girls to answer their felt needs and wants.
- Extension is teaching people what to want, as well as how to work out ways of satisfying their wants and inspiring them to achieve their desires.
- Extension is teaching through 'learning by doing' and 'seeing is believing'.
- Extension is working in harmony with the culture of the people.
- Extension is a two way channel; it brings scientific information to village people and it also takes the problems of the village people to the scientific institutions for solution.

3. Differentiate between formal education and extension education
Formal Education

1. Theory taught first then works up to practicals
2. Fixed curriculum
3. Authority rests with the teacher
4. Class Attendance is compulsory

5. Teaching is mainly vertical
6. Homogenous audience
7. It is rigid

Extension Education

1. Starts with practical theory later
2. No fixed curriculum
3. Authority rests with the people
4. Participation is voluntary
5. Teaching is mainly horizontal
6. Large and heterogenous audience
7. It is flexible

4. Extension teaching methods

- **a. Individual method**
- In this method, the extension worker contact the target people or learner individually. the essence of this particular contact method. it helps to create a greater interpersonal communication and face to face contact hence good rapport between the extension worker and the target people.
- **b. Group method**
- This teaching method is used to contact a group of people, which comprises of 5 persons to a maximum of 50 persons. This method helps to motivate the people in a group to accept change. It is comparatively less expensive and has more coverage.
- **c. Mass method**
- This kind of extension teaching method is used for the dissemination of information to a heterogeneous mass of people. In such a method, no face to face contact is found. This method is suitable for creating general awareness and large number of people may be communicated within a short time.

5. Explain Home Science Extension

- Home science extension is an applied science which aims at bringing about change in the behaviour of the target groups through dissemination of scientific and technical information in the areas of

Home Science.

- Home Science Extension is concerned with teaching, research and extension which are the functions of the Universities and institutes of research, extension and higher learning.
- Home Science Extension service performs the task of bridging the gap between research centres and home-makers by working as a linkage between the institutions of higher learning and the organisations for home makers.

6. Explain the Role of home science extension in national development

- Dissemination of information relating to advanced technology in agricultural production, which includes the use of improved seeds, methods of the use of chemical fertilizers, application of advanced scientific knowledge to the farms and homes of the rural people.
- Scientific management of land based farming such as horticulture, sericulture, dairying, poultry etc, by the farming community; overall improvement of the quality of life of the rural people within the framework of the national economic and social policies as a whole.
- The eradication of extreme poverty and hunger, promotion of gender eqality and the empowerment of women combating HIV/AIDS, malaria and other diseases, and ensuring environmental sustainability.
- It equips the future citizens with relevant knowledge and competence, and prepares them to become efficient custodians of the nation's future.

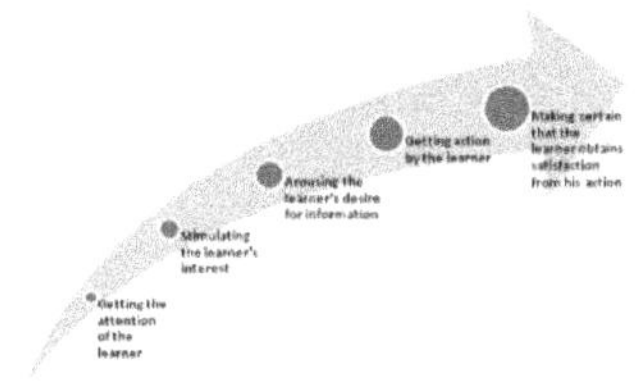

Steps in extension teaching

CHAPTER XII

Communication in Home Science Extension

1 Mark Questions and Answers

1. Enlist the elements of communication

Sender ---------- Message --------- Treatment---------- Channel--------- Receiver

2. Which of the following is not an element of communication

Kinesics (b) Sender (c) Channel (d) Treatment

3. Find out the first element of communication. (**Sender**)

4. A type of communication is communication that is neither written nor verbal. **(Non verbal)**

5. Which of the following is not an objective of communication

(a) Information (b) Empathy (c) Influencing (d) **Job satisfaction**

6. One of the following is not a function of communication

a) Persuasion b) **Pastexperience** c) Education d) Information

7. Give any one objective of communication. (**Information**)

8. Complete it: Sender, Message, Treatment, Channel, ... ? (**Receiver**)

9. Find out the correct order.

(a) **Sender ® Message ® Treatment ® Channel ® Receiver.**

(b) Sender ® Channel ® Treatment ® Message ® Receiver.

(c) Message ® Sender ® Treatment ® Receiver ® Channel.

(d) Message ® Channel ® Sender ® Receiver ® Treatment.

10. Dale's cone of experience was proposed by .... **(Edgard Dale)**

• • •

Short Answer Questions and Answers

1. Define Communication

Communication is a process by which two or more people exchange facts, ideas, feelings or impressions in ways that each gain a common understanding of meaning, intent and use of message.

2. What do you mean by contrived experiences?

Contrived experiences are edited copies of reality and are used as substitutes for real things when it is not practical or not possible to bring or do the real thing in the classroom. These include models, mock ups, specimens, simulations and games.

3. Explain the different types of communication on the basis of expression

- **Verbal communication** - Communication with words is called verbal communication, which can be written, oral or visual.
- **Non verbal communication** - Non verbal communication is communication that is neither written nor verbal. Non verbal communication refers to the communication of messages without the use of words. Communication based on physical gestures, facial expressions, and other non verbal cues is known as non verbal communication.

4. State the objectives of communication.

- Human relations: Communication is to help and promote human relations. There can be no mutual understanding without communication.
- Empathy: Empathy is the ability to feel and share another person's emotions.
- Persuasion: It is a process of convincing and motivating a person to get things done. Speech is one of the methods to persuade a person.
- Information: In the new information order of the world, information transmission is the process of getting things done.
- Influencing: Communication is aimed at influencing, persuading, motivating or activating towards desired goals.
- Understanding: Mutual understanding is another objective of communication.

5. Explain the importance of communication.

- **Coordination**: An effective system of communication promotes better coordination among people and organisations. It helps a lot in coordination.
- **Smooth working**: If the messages are not flowing freely across the organisation, smooth functioning and unrestricted working of the organisation is not possible.

- **Effective decision making**: Problem defining, alternative courses of action, selection of the best course of action are all possible only with necessary information supplied to the decision maker.
- **Cooperation**: Cooperation among workers, collective or joint efforts, are possible only with the exchange of information between individuals and groups. The two way communication network develops co-operation between people.
- **Effective leadership**: Communication is the basis for direction, motivation as well as establishment of effective leadership. It is through the medium of communication that the followers convey their opinions, ideas, feelings, facts etc to their leader.

6. Briefly explain the functions of Communication

- **Persuasion function**: Persuasion is the ability to change the attitude or behaviour of the target audience.
- **Interaction function**: Coordination among group and people, sharing of knowledge about activities and programmes
- **Information function**: Communication can help in rapid access to needed information at different levels in understandable form.
- **Entertainment function**: Folk media, electronic and print media etc. help in transmitting the rich cultural heritage.

7. Differentiate between contrived experiences and dramatized experiences.

- Contrived experiences are edited copies of reality and are used as substitutes for real things when it is not practical or not possible to bring or do the real thing in the classroom. Examples are models, mock ups, specimens, simulations and games.
- Dramatised experiences are process of communication in which both participants and spectators are engaged. A creative reaction and sharing of ideas take place. eg. dramas, puppet shows, tableau, role playing, pantomime, pageants.

6 Marks Questions and Answers

8. Classify Verbal communication

The medium of verbal communication is chiefly of three types.

- **Oral communication:** It is the communication using speech or talking that is understood by all parties. Verbal communication is used most often and is popular in the form of speeches and group discussions.
- **Written communication:** Written communication includes notices, letters and anything else that can be put into written words and symbols. The advantage of written communication is that it is tangible, lasting and controllable.
- **Visual communication** - It is communication through a visual aid. Information is presented or expressed with two dimensional images, like signs, drawings, graphic design, illustrations, animation etc.

9. Explain the factors influencing communication.

a. **Attitude:** The attitude of a person towards the given situation is influenced by the peers, parents, environment, life experiences, perception and intellectual processes.
b. **Socio cultural background:** Various cultures and ethnic groups display different communication patterns
c. **Knowledge of subject matter:** A person who is well educated or knowledgeable about certain topics may communicate with others at a high level of understanding.
d. **Environmental factors:** Environmental factors such as time, place, number of people present, and noise level can influence communication between people in that particular surrounding.

10. Briefly explain the Dale's cone of experience

Direct, purposeful experiences: Learning by doing is the best type of learning. Actual experience is very effective in learning.eg. making a piece of furniture, cultivating any crop.

2. **Contrived experiences:** Contrived experiences are edited copies of reality and are used as substitutes for real things when it is not practical or not possible to bring or do the real thing in the classroom. These include models, mock ups, specimens, simulations and games.
3. **Dramatised experiences:** It is essentially a process of communication in which both participants and spectators are engaged. eg. dramas, puppet shows, tableau, role playing, pantomime, pageants.

4. **Demonstrations:** Demonstrations help to visualize a process that might be difficult to understand completely only through verbal description. There are three types of demonstration; Method, Result and Composite Demonstrations.
5. **Field trips:** During field trips the learner acquires first hand and direct experience of the existing situation through observation.
6. **Exhibits:** Exhibits are systematic representations of the reality. These are only seen, therefore positioned at less effective source in cone of experience.
7. **Motion pictures/ Television:**mTelevision has been universally acclaimed as the powerful medium of mass communication. Television and motion pictures can reconstruct the reality of the past so effectively that we are made to feel we are there.
8. **Recordings, radio and still pictures:** Radio is suitable for creating general awareness among people, help them change their attitude and reinforce learning. Recordings are done on disc, tape or wire. Still pictures can be projected or non- projected.
9. **Visual symbols:** These consist of a device used to assist teaching by visible means, in order to create an impression of realism in the learner's mind. Examples are charts, graphs, maps, and diagrams.
10. **Verbal Symbols:** Verbal symbols are least effective in terms of learning among learners. Words and spoken language is less interesting than all other methods. That is why these are placed at the pinnacle of the cone of experience.

11. Illustrate Dales cone of experience

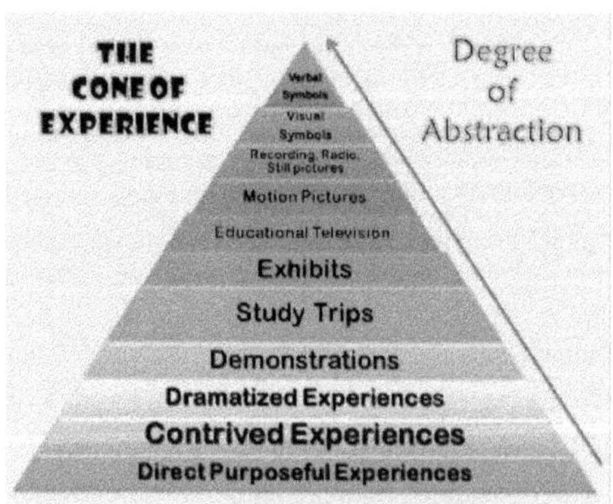

References

Home Science, class XII (Textbook), State Council of Educational Research and Training (SCERT), KERALA 2015

www.ingramcontent.com/pod-product-compliance
Lightning Source LLC
LaVergne TN
LVHW021158160826
845679LV00024B/2158

* 9 7 9 8 8 9 4 7 5 4 2 3 9 *